PRAISE FOR

"I have known Matt Doherty well since we played against each other in college. Matt was a fantastic player, an outstanding coach, a fierce competitor, and he has always been a person of integrity. When he faced adversity, he fought, overcame, persevered, and grew to be the thoughtful leader he is today. Matt is everything you could ask for in a friend and leader."

—JAY BILAS, ESPN

"I've known Matt since he was a senior in high school in Long Island. I helped recruit him and helped coach him at North Carolina, and he was on my coaching staff at Kansas for seven successful seasons. He's always been a very intelligent person, player and coach, and the many experiences he shares in *REBOUND*, including how to deal with both successes and adversity, will help anyone in a leadership position."

—ROY WILLIAMS, Head Coach, University of North Carolina

"I've always been a big believer in everything Matt touches. Shortly after playing a key role on UNC's 1982 National Championship team, he worked for us at CBS as a stage manager on our college basketball broadcasts. He is pure class. And he understands the ebb and flow of a life well lived."

—JIM NANTZ, CBS Sports Commentator

"Highly recommend Matt Doherty's new book as he has tasted victory as a player and coach, but has also dealt with being on the top in coaching to falling off the coaching tree. He has rebounded in the Game of Life by utilizing all the skills that were vital in formulating his career. You will learn so much from Matt's views on dealing with your mental attitude. Yes, the book is Awesome Baby!

—**DICK VITALE**, ESPN, Basketball Hall of Fame

"Matt Doherty knows about rebounding on the court and in life. His journey and experiences are inspiring."

—**CHARLES BARKLEY**, Basketball Hall of Fame, and Emmy Award Winner

"Powerful. Inspirational. Real. Matt Doherty chose to turn his 'Pain into Passion' and now he infuses wisdom, insight and practical advice from lessons learned to benefit all of us. A fascinating look inside the life of an extraordinary man. It's a must-read!"

—**JON GORDON**, best-selling author of *The Power of Positive Leadership*

"Matt's leadership and understanding of sport has also connected him with friends and family to help mentor and guide them through the worst and best of times. He truly understands every member of the team which enables those around him to achieve greatness."

—**KENNY SMITH**, NBA Champion and TNT NBA Studio Analyst

"A riveting read. This book is incredibly empowering. Matt Doherty draws from his own life journey to teach and instill in others the confidence to trust in ourselves—even when life hits a bump in the road."

—**KEVIN PRITCHARD**, President, Basketball Operations, Indiana Pacers

"To be sure, this book is honest, real, and gracefully told. Matt's story is a rousing read for all who aspire to succeed."

—**KEVIN M. WHITE**, Vice President and Director of Athletics, Duke University

"In basketball, a championship team needs a great rebounder. A rebounder is defined as a player who retrieves the ball and gains possession after a missed shot. Matt Doherty retrieved the ball and gained possession of his life. In the battle of life, Matt is someone you would want in your foxhole. His life story clearly tells you why."

—**BOB MCKILLOP**, Head Coach, Davidson College Basketball, Atlantic 10 Conference

"Matt Doherty helps take us from here to there, from setback to comeback. Few of us find we are on a linear roadmap to the top, and we can learn much from the revival of others to get back on track if momentarily derailed. *REBOUND* is a compelling account for doing so, wonderfully brought to life by Matt's own fall and personal renewal."

—**MICHAEL USEEM**, Professor of Management at the Wharton School, University of Pennsylvania, and author of *The Leadership Moment* and co-author of *Mastering Catastrophic Risk*

"*REBOUND* walks us through one persons successes and challenges in life as a basketball player and coach. A compelling reading but that's not the point—Matt Doherty shares his personal journey to teach others the valuable lessons learned from his successes and failures. I could not put the book down!"

—**MITCH KUPCHAK**, President of Basketball Operations & General Manager, Charlotte Hornets

"Life is full of challenges and opportunities. Matt provides insight into both by sharing his personal accounts of his successes and his failures. We all experience events that change our lives, and his thoughts about the lessons he has learned are valuable."

—**BUBBA CUNNINGHAM**, Director of Athletics, The University of North Carolina

"As someone who has also experienced life's highs and lows, I found Matt's reflections upon his own journey to be most valuable. In chapter after chapter this good man uses his life's experiences ranging from the highs of winning a National Championship to the lows of losing his job to teach others how to overcome and persevere and become a better, stronger leader. I highly recommend reading *Rebound: From Pain to Passion*."

—**ERSKINE BOWLES**, Former White House Chief of Staff

"The people with whom Matt has played, coached and worked as a player, coach and administrator, and his love for the game, have given him a unique perspective into what it means to be a leader."

—**DAN GAVITT**, NCAA Senior Vice President of Basketball

"If you are a fan of basketball and a fan of life, you will become of fan of Matt Doherty when you read *Rebound: From Pain to Passion*. Luckily for me, I have been a friend AND fan of Matt Doherty for a very long time. This book will inspire and make you think because the stories and leadership lessons are fabulous."

—**FRAN FRASCHILLA**, ESPN

"Throughout *REBOUND* Coach Doherty shows us many great lessons on how to lead. One underlying yet important lesson is that the distance from being an individual talent to becoming an effective leader is long, but can be traveled by diligent desire, learning, and practice."

—**DR. GERALD BELL**, Bell Leadership Institute

"Mister Cool! #44—Matt and I came in together as freshman—introduced to each other and never looked back! Excited to have another New Yorker along with Jimmy Black. With the style of play you had to be clever with the ball, especially playin' in the ACC. Matt was a savvy and efficient passer; sort of a perfectionist. His assists were on point. I see why Coach Smith recruited him. It made our team more diverse at guard with his play and ability to read defenses. He definitely was a student of the game. Wouldn't define him as a role player, but without him we wouldn't have been as successful."

—**SAM PERKINS**, Former UNC star and NBA player

"Matt was not only an awesome teammate and brother, but he will always be my brother for life. He has always been very well read, and thoroughly researches anything he is working on. As a player he was always prepared which showed on many levels. The same can be said and applied to his leadership book."

—**JIMMY BLACK**, Captain of UNC's 1982 National Champion team

"I've known Matt for many years. Matt has a unique and authoritative toughness and discipline about him. He never makes excuses and always looks for solutions. In fact, if I where a GM in the NBA looking for a gifted leader and coach, Matt would be my first choice."

—**BRAD DAUGHERTY**, 5 time NBA All-STAR , College Basketball All American. ESPN and NBC Sports Analyst

"Matt Doherty has shared his inspiring personal leadership journey and offers all readers insights into surmounting setbacks and leading with vision, courage and passion. His is an engaging story and must read for those who are committed to using their influence to help others achieve success and realize their potential."

—**CAROL C. WEBER**, Visiting Professor Emeritus, Darden Graduate School of Business, University of Virginia

"Coach Doherty taught me that being a leader isn't an end-state, but a journey. Post-UNC, he seriously studied and invested in growing as a leader, and I was a huge beneficiary."

—**JON KILLEN**, Former SMU Captain

"I was extremely fortunate to play for Matt at Kansas University and then work for him as an Assistant Coach. Matt is a unique combination of competitiveness, organization, compassion, evaluation (self and player), creative thinking and adaptability that had a tremendous impact on me as a player and future head coach. There is a presence, personality but most importantly a growth mindset that makes him a great leader that will brings a wealth of knowledge and experience that he can share. I don't know where I would be in my basketball journey if I hadn't had the opportunity to learn from him. There is no doubt you will enjoy and learn from all that he has in this book."

—**REX WALTERS**, Kansas All-American, Former college coach, NBA Coach

"What you read here is the true and authentic Matt Doherty. He is as you will read, a deeply reflective, always striving to be a better man, father, husband and coach. In *REBOUND* he does us the honor of sharing his story that includes great highs and unimaginable lows. *REBOUND* tells the seventeen year story of a man who has been in the epicenter of Final Four basketball, booted out, and who through the hard work of self-awareness, found his way back to his own grounded joy of the game. The best leaders are those who suffered and cared enough to figure out what there was to learn. Matt Doherty is a learner through and through—and a great note taker which is why this book is a riveting read and a practical guide for any leader starting a new position."

—**FRANCES JOHNSTON, PH.D.**, world-renowned scholar-practitioner, Founder, Teleos Leaders, and co-author of the Harvard Business Press book, *Becoming a Resonant Leader*

"I have known Matt for more than 20 years and the most impressive thing about him is his thirst to improve. He always wants to get better every day. While it is a great talking point that he won a National Championship in 1982 and was the 2001 NCAA Coach of the Year, what is more important is how he has continued to learn and better himself. We had Matt speak to our partners (more than 200 people attended) and he got rave reviews from the presentation. It is not often that you have the opportunity to hear from someone who has achieved success, but is willing to, and more importantly, openly discuss their failures. The opportunity for our partners and my employees to hear his thoughts about leadership in ways that reflected both successes and failures is what makes the talk real and authentic, and is why it was so impactful."

—**MALCOLM K. FARMER**, President & General Manager, Texas Legends

"What defines you in life is not when things are going well but how you handle your life in the face of adversity defines your character, strength and who you truly are."
—**RAYMOND FELTON**, Former UNC star and current NBA player

"Coach Doherty recruited me out of Indiana, I trusted him and his staff with my future. To this day I don't regret that decision. Although things didn't work out at UNC for Coach Doherty, he and staff always tried to help us reach our dreams and goals, and for that I will always respect him."

—**SEAN MAY**, Former UNC star and current UNC Assistant Coach

"In the game of basketball there are times when the ball bounces your way and then there are times when it doesn't. The same can be said about life. I've known Matt Doherty for over 20 years and in his new book *Rebound: From Pain to Passion*, Matt does a great job sharing his unique story and detailing the 'bounces' that he's had in life. We can all learn from his experiences, which can help us to handle the 'bounces' we will face in our lives."

—**RYAN HUMPHREY**, Former Notre Dame star and current Notre Dame assistant

"Coach Matt Doherty challenged me everyday as player and young man at the University of Notre Dame. He instilled a toughness and belief in me that carried me through 10 years as an NBA player. Coach D has been a coach, mentor and friend that has taught me so much through his own successes and failures. He shares these valuable life lessons in *REBOUND!*"

—**MATT CARROLL**, Former Notre Dame star and NBA player

"When Matt Doherty became the head coach at the University of Notre Dame, he gave me a chance to leave an impression. He challenged me. He pushed me. His passion inspired me. His drive and energy made me want to run through walls for him and my team. That is what leadership is all about to me."

—**JIMMY DILLON**, 2000 captain of the Notre Dame basketball team and current Director of Hoops 24-7 (Phil. PA)

REBOUND
FROM PAIN TO PASSION

Leadership Lessons Learned

Matt Doherty

SPORTS
PUBLISHING
GROUP★★★★★

Rebound

©2021 by Matt Doherty

Published by Sports Publishing Group, Franklin, TN.

Cover Photo by Kathleen Martin

Edited by David Brown

Cover and Interior Design by Suzanne Lawing

Printed in the United States of America

ISBN: 978-1-7340850-1-3

ACKNOWLEDGEMENTS

I am grateful to so many people for their encouragement, input and influence along the way. Not only in writing this book, but impacting my life. Writing this book has been a walk down memory lane from my days growing up on Long Island to playing at UNC to coaching college basketball to learning from great leadership experts.

I was blessed with a great family surrounded by a supportive community that encouraged me to chase my dreams. Coaches, teammates and competitors that pushed me and instructed me. Friends and family that shared in wonderful experiences that created memories and friendships that last a lifetime.

The foundation coaches Bob McKillop and Dick Zeitler gave me in high school prepared me well for my career at North Carolina. The toughness and fundamentals learned from them and my teammates helped me make a seamless transition to play at the best program in college basketball. I was blessed to be coached by one of the best coaches in all team sports, legendary Coach Dean Smith. The staff of Bill Guthridge, Eddie Fogler and Roy Williams were amazing teachers and men. It was a dream come true playing for them at UNC and with some of basketball's all-time great players. Al Wood, Jimmy Black, James Worthy, Sam Perkins, Michael Jordan, Brad Daugherty and Kenny Smith were fantastic players, wonderful teammates and talented players.

Your life is a series of decisions and dealing with the consequences. The better decisions you make the better your life will be. The decision to attend Holy Trinity High School and the University of North Carolina were two of the best decisions I ever made. I am a proud Titan and Tar Heel.

I decided to become a coach because I wanted to impact young men the way my coaches impacted me. The lessons you learn playing a team sport for quality coaches goes way beyond the court. They are life lessons that you can draw upon in most any circumstance in business and life.

My leadership journey started after I was forced to resign from UNC in 2003. John Black encouraged me to take this journey and coached me along the way. Carol and Jack Weber taught me valuable leadership lessons at the Darden School. Fran Johnston and Mike Useem did the same at The Wharton School. Dr. Jerry Bell was very generous with his time devoted to helping me become a better leader.

Thanks to John Black and Scott Stankavage for reviewing, editing and encouraging me with this project. Their support is what friends are made of.

To all the coaches that touched my life and all the teammates I had from grammar school to college. To all the players I was blessed to coach. Thank you!

Publisher Larry Carpenter came highly recommended by Scott and he has been a pro. He laid out a plan and kept me on track during the process.

Publicist Cindy Birne was a rock star. Her enthusiasm and passion is unmatched. She attacked the project and made me feel that we could do something special.

Thanks to photographer Kathleen Martin for making me look good on the cover. That was a challenge!

To my parents, my sisters and my brother. Thank you. How lucky was I to grow up in the Doherty household in East Meadow, NY.

To Bobby Ellington, thank you for always being there.

Lastly, Kelly, Tucker and Hattie. You have been on the roller coaster with me. We have had high highs and low lows, but such is life. Your love and support is truly appreciated. I love you all very much!

"In the world you will have tribulation.
But take heart; I have overcome the world."
- JOHN 16:33 ESV

FOREWORD

In 1981, I entered the University of North Carolina as a skinny freshman people called Mike Jordan. Matt Doherty was more worldly and mature and had been around the block already: he was a sophomore. Our coach, of course, was the legendary Dean Smith.

Coach Smith was a great man who preached loyalty and teamwork—his vaunted "Carolina Way." All of us who played at North Carolina have a deep connection, and one that goes even deeper for those of us who played together. It's a brotherhood. For Matt and me, it was even stronger. Our parents bonded, too. Whether it was down in Chapel Hill for home games or on the road, Matt's parents and my parents would always get together for meals and just had a great relationship.

From our earliest practices at North Carolina, I could see that Matt was a leader. He was smart, methodical, and fundamentally sound. He might not have been the most physically gifted player on the team, but he was always two steps ahead of his more athletic teammates because of the way he could see the game.

We started out my freshman year as the pre-season number one team in the country. That led to one of the only times Matt beat me out at something: appearing on the cover of *Sports Illustrated* for the first time—he, along with Coach Smith, Jimmy Black, Sam Perkins, and James Worthy appeared on the cover of the magazine's College Basketball Preview issue.

As a freshman, Coach wouldn't let me join the upperclassmen on the cover.

Once the season began, it was a whirlwind navigating being away from home, juggling classes and practice, and learning to play with the eyes of the country on us. Throughout that year, I admired Matt's steady leadership, his positive outlook, and his calmness under pressure. He showed that poise when he sank three crucial free throws in our win over Virginia in the 1982 ACC Championship Game. We went on to beat Georgetown in the NCAA Championship Game a few weeks later.

Matt challenged me each and every day. He helped teach me how to really think about the game of basketball, not just use my skills to play. He didn't make many mistakes, he truly understood the game, and was like a coach on the floor. Because of Matt, I became a better player. I valued his approach and came to think of him as a mini Dean Smith (even though Matt was a good bit taller than Coach).

It's no surprise to me that Matt is training the next generation of leaders through his Doherty Coaching Practice. After all, he was training his teammates, including me, all those years ago on the court at UNC.

-Michael Jordan

PREFACE

In *Rebound: From Pain to Passion,* I will share stories from my career as a head coach at Notre Dame and North Carolina. Stories of good moments and bad moments. My hope is that you will use this book as a reference to help you navigate the rough seas of leadership through life and business. Whether coaching a sport, running a company, or leading your family, there are skills that can be developed to put you and your organization in position for success!

I was blessed to have played college basketball at the University of North Carolina for the great coach Dean Smith and worked under legendary coaches Roy Williams at Kansas and Bob McKillop at Davidson College. I have been a part of many successful teams in high school and college that have gone on to win national championships, state championships, and conference titles. I played with great players who went on to stellar NBA careers. Players like James Worthy, Sam Perkins, Michael Jordan, Brad Daugherty, and Kenny Smith. I learned many lessons that I used as a head coach at Notre Dame and UNC. However, my journey has been anything but smooth. I failed and dealt with the pain of losing my job in a very public forum. As a result, I questioned my leadership abilities.

In 1999, I was named head coach at the University of Notre Dame. As an Irish Catholic kid from Long Island, being at Notre Dame was an unbelievable fit. I loved Notre Dame, the players, my staff, and the administration. We had a terrific season. I anticipated being there for a long time, but in June 2000, Bill Guthridge retired as the head coach at UNC. Roy Williams was expected to replace Coach Guthridge, but he turned down the opportunity to return to Chapel Hill. UNC then turned to me. Dean Smith recruited me to come "home" with the help of Michael Jordan. I ended up taking the job!

In 2001, we won the ACC Regular Season Championship and I was named AP National Coach of the Year. I was on the fast track to becoming a great coach at one of the most prestigious programs in college basketball.

Two short years later, I was forced to resign!

After losing my job, I had a decision to make. I could become bitter or I could work to get better! I chose to get better. I went on a leadership journey to "Learn and Grow" that I will detail in the following chapters.

I hope this book will have a positive impact on your life.

CHAPTER ONE:

LOVE OF THE GAME

*"Passion is energy. Feel the power that comes
from focusing on what excites you."*
—OPRAH WINFREY

I grew up in East Meadow, NY, a small, middle-class town
about thirty miles from New York City. My dad owned a Pepsi
route. He would get up every morning at 6 a.m. and commute
to "The City" for twenty-five years. Rain or snow, "Big Walt,"
as he was fondly known, would make his way to work. At the
plant in Long Island City, he would load up his truck and then
drive through New York's Midtown Tunnel to deliver soda
in Greenwich Village. My dad grew up in Brooklyn and was
a great athlete, but never really discussed it. He ran track at
La Salle Academy in Manhattan and went on to play minor
league baseball. His baseball career took him from Canada to
South Carolina. Walt Doherty was a pitcher hoping to make it
to the big leagues. My mother grew up in the Bronx. She was
a pretty lady who loved family, friends, and her Irish heritage.
Her parents came to the United States from Dingle in County

Kerry, Ireland, and settled in NYC where they were superintendents in an apartment building.

My parents loved each other and their five children. After the birth of my older sisters, Meg and Nan, my parents moved to Long Island where they had three more children: Maureen, myself, and John. We were blue collar middle class. Growing up on the south shore of Nassau County was a wonderful place to be raised. As a young boy, I had parks, beaches, access to The City, and wonderful teams to root for. I was a NY Mets fan, and tried to pitch like Tom Seaver. I was a NY Knicks fan, and tried to play like Bill Bradley. I was a NY Giants fan, and tried to throw like Fran Tarkenton. I was a NY Rangers fan, and tried to play goalie like Eddie Giacomin. There was a sport for every season, and I played them all.

Like most young boys on Long Island, I started playing baseball. My dad would throw with me in our large backyard. I remember crouching down like a catcher and he would pitch to me. He could throw a knuckleball that would dance across the plate. Every once in a while, he would throw a "fastball," and my glove would pop and my hand would sting! Even after a long day delivering soda, my dad would be happy to play catch. I never remember seeing my dad in a bad mood and he never pushed me to play sports. I was blessed.

When I was in fourth grade, my dad signed me up for Gus Alfieri's All-American Basketball Camp. Coach Alfieri was a great high school coach at St. Anthony's HS on Long Island. As we prepared for the week of camp, I vividly remember my dad taking me to Nescott Drugs to buy my first jockstrap! Afterwards, we sat in the car, and he said to me, "When a coach is correcting you, don't say, 'I know.'" Wow. What wisdom. My dad was teaching me how to be coachable. Many years later, I would pass that nugget on to my son, Tucker.

I loved camp, every minute of it. I was learning and getting better. Each day, we would have a guest speaker. I would always sit in the front row, so if they asked for someone to demonstrate, I would raise my hand and run out onto the court. One day, Julius Erving spoke at camp. "Dr. J" was a great player for the NY Nets at the time. They played in Nassau Coliseum, only five miles from my home. Here was Dr. J at the All-American Camp giving a clinic on ... pivoting! The best dunker of all time was giving a clinic on pivoting! When he asked for ten campers to demonstrate, I sprinted off the floor to join him! Dr. J then proceeded to teach us how to front pivot and reverse pivot. It was a very fundamental drill that could be considered boring, but I loved it ... and I used it with every team I ever coached.

When I would get home each night from camp, I was exhausted, but I would go to my room and write down notes on what I learned that day. I was, and still am, a note taker. I wanted to be able to reference my notes from camp so I could continue to improve as a player long after camp was over. The thing I loved most about basketball was that I didn't need anyone else to improve. I could work on my game by myself to get better. In football and baseball, you needed others to work with to get better.

In sixth grade, I read a lot of books about sports. I remember reading a book about "Pistol Pete" Maravich and how he always worked on his game. He would dribble a basketball everywhere he went, even in the movie theater! "Pistol" would shoot the ball to himself in his bed and he would sleep with a basketball. I ended up doing the same!

I was still playing baseball at the time, and I remember reading Bill Bradley's book *Life on the Run*. He said, "If you are not working on your game and someone else is, when you two meet, the other player will have the advantage." Right then, I decided to quit baseball! I loved basketball so much that I wanted to have the advantage when I went up against other players.

I need to note that I never had any pushback from my father when I made that decision. Even though he was a minor league baseball player, he never pushed me to play baseball. That was a lesson I took to raising my two children, Tucker and Hattie.

Prospect Park in Nassau County was three blocks from my house. This was heaven for me. There were two full basketball courts, a huge swimming pool, tennis courts, and paddle ball courts. The best players in Nassau County played there. Dr. J would show up, along with other NBA and ABA players like Kevin Joyce, Dennis DuVal, Jim O'Brien, Marc Iavaroni, and Len Kosmalski. Great local players who played at St. John's, Hofstra, Princeton, Tennessee, South Carolina, and C.W. Post would compete nightly. Some of the best high school players from Long Island would play, too. Players from Holy Trinity, Chaminade, St. Agnes, East Meadow, Hempstead, and Roosevelt. Then there were the local players that every park had in New York. Players who weren't household names, but they were damn good players, players who would have a "go-to move" that you couldn't stop. I would try to mimic and incorporate those moves into my game. Lastly, there were the guys who gave each park in NY character. Guys with the nicknames like "House of Pain," "Snake," and "The Doctor."

The big event of each day would be on Court 1 at 6 p.m. I made a deal with my family that I wouldn't have to clean up after dinner so I could ride my bike to "The Park" to try to get into the first game. I would be filled with excitement as I would ride the three blocks in anticipation of who would show up. What great player would be there? Would I get in the first game? Would we string some wins together?

As a sixth grader, I was out of my league, but I didn't care. I wanted to play with and against the best. I knew if I played against the best, I would have a big advantage when I would play against kids my age during the school year at St. Raphael's. There I was, this skinny sixth grader playing on Court 1 with and against the best players in Nassau County at Prospect Park! The games were intense. Call your own fouls. Games to 11 points. Lose and you sit. And if I lost, I would be done playing on Court 1 because I wasn't good enough to get picked up by the next team ... or the team after that ... or the team after that! There were often five "nexts." "Next" was the person who had the rights to the next game. He would pick the best players not playing, and may save a spot or two for the best players who lost the previous game. If my team lost, my options were to find a game on Court 2 or watch the great players compete on Court 1.

What did I learn at The Park?

I learned about meritocracy. Meritocracy is defined as a system in which the talented are chosen and moved ahead on the basis of their achievement. Skin color didn't matter. Income didn't matter. Your ability to help a team win ... that's all that mattered!

I learned about playing a role. As a young player, I wasn't the best player on the court, so I had to do the little things to help us win. If I didn't know how to fit in on a team with older guys, I would never get to play with them again.

I learned to listen and be coachable. I was blessed to be around veteran players who took the time to give me instruction. Whether they barked at me on the court or quietly gave me instruction between games, I soaked it all up. If I didn't listen, the older guys wouldn't want me on their team.

I learned to compete. If you lost at The Park, you sat! And if I didn't play hard, I would get abused by the older players. "Point game" was when one team needed just one basket to win. You could feel the intensity rise on the court. Each player cut harder, screened harder, and defended harder. There were no easy baskets when it was "point game" because nobody wanted to lose. Nobody wanted to sit.

I learned toughness. At The Park, you had to fight. Fight for position, fight for the ball, fight for the win, or just plain fight. It was all about respect! As a boy, I often took a physical beating at The Park playing against older players, some of them men. However, I wouldn't show them I was hurt because I wanted their respect. If you weren't tough, you didn't belong on Court 1.

I learned that you are only as good as your last game. There were nights when our team would win five games in a row and it might be 9:30 p.m. The Park closed at 10 p.m. The guys might say, "Last game." If you lost that last game, you felt bad. That left a terrible taste in my mouth. No matter how many games you win, you are only as good as the last one. You have to fight human nature. It is easy to relax in that situation, but I learned to dig in and compete so I could leave The Park as a winner!

I learned to dream. Often, I would be at The Park on a Saturday morning by myself after watching the Knicks play on TV the night before. I would imagine playing in Madison Square Garden as a Knick. As I dribbled the ball, I would say to myself, "Frazier brings up the ball and passes to Monroe. Monroe to Bradley. Bradley probes the defense and passes to DeBusschere. DeBusschere throws into Reed. Reed kicks it out to Bradley. 3 ... 2 ... Bradley shoots ... aaahhhhhh! It's good at the buzzer!" If I missed the shot, it would be the end of the half. If I made the jumper, it was the end of the game and there was a big celebration!

I made a deal with my parents back then. I didn't want a summer job that would take me away from The Park. I remember telling them that my summer job was basketball, and that if I worked on my game, I would get a college scholarship. That "summer job" paid off! However, I did have a paper route. First, I delivered Newsday, but that was an afternoon paper that I had to deliver after school. During the spring and fall, the local high school players would meet at The Park about 3:30 p.m. When I delivered Newsday, I would miss out on that competition, so I started delivering the Daily News before school.

On Long Island, I was blessed with great coaching. Many men were first-generation Long Islanders, having grown up in The City. The Coleman brothers coached me at St. Raphael's grammar school. They were terrific coaches. My 8th grade team won the Nassau County Championship in 1976. The starting point guard was Gene Larkin who went on to play baseball at Columbia and for the world champion Minnesota Twins!

I attended summer camps and played on summer teams and area select teams that were coached by men like Rev. Ed Visscher of Lutheran HS, Howie Frankel, Gus Alfieri, Bob Kenney of Herricks HS, Frank Morris of St. Agnes ... the list goes on. So many men invested in teaching me the beautiful game of basketball, along with sharing life lessons that helped me grow as a player and person.

Bob McKillop was the coach at Holy Trinity HS at the time. My sisters, Nan and Maureen, attended "Trinity," and I would often attend their basketball games. I remember seeing great games there. Those games were intense with packed crowds. That stoked my dreams of playing in that environment one day. Malcolm Cesare was a star player at Holy Trinity and ended up playing at the University of Florida. He was a 6-9 forward who could shoot and score. The big rival was St. Agnes of Rockville Centre. Malcolm had thirty-nine points in the league championship game at Hofstra in a loss to St. Agnes. The place was packed. Mike Palma was the star for St. Agnes, and he ended up playing at Wake Forest before transferring to Iona College where he played for Jim Valvano. I remember being upset when Holy Trinity lost. As I came out of the bleachers, Mike Palma was cutting down the nets. I reached into my pocket where there were a few Tootsie Rolls left from a big bag that I consumed during the contest. I grabbed a Tootsie Roll and fired it at Palma! Fortunately, I missed. I hated St. Agnes!

Paul Eibeler was a friend of Nan's, and he was a good player at Holy Trinity before attending Loyola College in Baltimore. Paul became my mentor. He took me under his wing. We would play one-on-one, run miles together, and do push-ups. Paul would take me in The City to play pick-up games and watch him in the Elmcor Summer League. He taught me how to work and improve. Paul is still a very close friend. I was blessed to have him as a friend and mentor.

My dreams included playing on the varsity as a freshman at Holy Trinity. No freshmen had ever done that before. I wanted to be the first. Bob McKillop was a tough, intense coach. I would often play with and against him at The Park. Whenever I was on the court with him, I was determined to impress him. However, he was not easily impressed. He never showed it, but that just drove me more.

My freshman year at Holy Trinity, I tried out for the varsity team. My parents were concerned about me being teammates with older players. How would I handle that socially? I begged them to allow me to try out, and they relented. Workouts were hard. "Mr. McKillop" worked us to exhaustion. I was a 6-4 freshman, but had no muscle and little hair on my body. I was going against what seemed to me as men. Guys with facial hair and muscles, but I loved every minute of it. Finally, Mr. McKillop posted the final roster on the locker room door. I remember walking by myself to see if my name was on the list. I walked up to the door and saw Mr. McKillop's impeccable handwriting. I went down the roster and I finally saw "Matt Doherty." I made the varsity!

My parents were quick to say, "Don't get a big head! Stay humble!"

CHAPTER TWO:

WINNING

*"Talent wins games, but teamwork
and intelligence win championships."*
—MICHAEL JORDAN

As a freshman at Holy Trinity, I came off the bench, but played in most every game. We had great players. Bob Testa, Jim Fearon, John Corso, and Mike Aldridge all went on to play in college. They were good to me. Bob would pick me up and drive me home from practice and games that first year. Mike did the same when I was a sophomore. We had great teams and won state and conference titles those first two years. I started as a sophomore and began to get recruiting letters from colleges. It was an exciting time.

After my sophomore year, Mr. McKillop decided to take an assistant coaching position at Davidson College. It was very concerning to me, as I loved playing for him and was anxious about who was going to fill his big shoes as our head coach. Holy Trinity ended up hiring Dick Zeitler. Mr. Zeitler played high school basketball for legendary coach Jack Curran at

Molloy before attending Georgetown. He was a great fit for our team. However, my junior year, we weren't as strong as previous teams. It was a frustrating year, as we didn't have the success we were accustomed to.

My senior year ended up being a storybook finish. We had great chemistry and Mr. Zeitler managed that group very well. Our school had become more diverse, as many students from large African American communities started to attend Holy Trinity. Our team was a mix of white and black players. That is one of the great things about sports. It brings people together from different backgrounds. We worked as a team and had great respect for each other, and "Coach Z" helped foster that. Our team was huge! By that time, I was 6-7. The other starters were Beau Ridley 6-7, Doug Poetzsch 6-6, along with guards Tim Devlin and Juan Rodriquez. Kenny Bantum 6-8 came off the bench. Beau played college ball at Elmira, Doug was a great player at Siena, Juan had a good career at Gannon, and Kenny became a great player at Cornell.

We started off great that season. I recall only losing one game, to powerhouse Mater Dei of NYC, by the time we rolled into January. Mater Dei had Vern Fleming who ended up playing at Georgia before going on to a long NBA career. Then one Friday in January, I was in school and had an itchy feeling on my body. I got home from school and saw some bumps on my body. I got out an encyclopedia, looked up "chickenpox," and saw, "A highly contagious viral infection causing an itchy, blister-like rash on the skin."

Uh-oh!

We were playing St. John the Baptist that night!

I immediately went into my parents' room, looked in the White Pages, picked up the rotary phone, and called Dr.

Schlifka's office. He was our family doctor. Pauline, the nurse, answered.

"Hello Pauline, are chickenpox going around?" I asked, getting right to the point.

Pauline said, "Yes!"

Uh-oh!

I asked, "What would happen if someone played a basketball game with chickenpox?"

Pauline responded, "You wouldn't want to do that!"

I said, "Well, what if you didn't know you had them and played a game? What would be the worst thing that could happen?"

Pauline answered, "Well … someone else might get it!"

"Okay! Thanks Pauline!" I said, and started preparing for the game!

That night, I put on a T-shirt to cover my shoulders, and went out and scored thirty-eight points in a nice home victory. Mission accomplished!

The next night, we were scheduled to play Lutheran HS. They were a powerhouse coached by … Mr. McKillop! Bob had returned to Long Island after one year at Davidson to take over for legendary high school coach Rev. Ed Visscher. I wanted to play in that game badly!

I remember waking up that Saturday morning and seeing that the chickenpox had spread. I walked downstairs and tried to casually walk into the kitchen. My dad was sitting in his normal spot at the head of the table facing me. My mother was at the sink. As I walked in, my mom and dad looked at me and paused. Then my dad stretched his arm up and pointed, saying, "Back to bed!" I pleaded with my parents to let me play that night, but to no avail! Back to bed I went. We lost to Lutheran and I ended up missing the next two games. We went 1-2 in that stretch and it killed me!

We went on to win the Catholic League Championship in an intense final game against rival St. Agnes at Hofstra. The gym was packed. It came down to the last possession. We held the ball for the last shot. I remember passing the ball to Tim Devlin on the right side in front of the St. Agnes bench. He passed it back to me, and St. Agnes' star, Audie Matthews, stepped in and almost stole the ball. I took the ball and dribbled toward the foul line, 3 … 2 … things went blank as I pulled up for a jump shot. The ball went through the net! St. Agnes called time-out with one second. We celebrated on the bench while Coach Z tried to calm us down. St. Agnes ended up trying a three-quarter court shot that missed. A big celebration ensued. We cut down the nets while the fans stormed the court! I got to cut down the net, as Mike Palma had done for St. Agnes on the same court only a few years before. I wonder if some young St. Agnes fan tried hitting me with a Tootsie Roll.

Dreams do come true.

We went on to win the State Championship in Rochester, NY, beating talented Adlai Stevenson HS with future college stars Freddie Brown (Georgetown) and Ed Pinckney (Villanova) in the semifinals.

Magical year!

CHAPTER THREE:

ACCEPTING THE CHALLENGE

"The key to life is accepting challenges.
Once someone stops doing this, he's dead."
—BETTE DAVIS

I was blessed to have great options in choosing a college. I received recruiting letters from programs all across the country. After my junior year of high school, I began to focus on four schools—Duke, Virginia, Notre Dame, and North Carolina. I really wanted to play in a big-time conference with a great college environment at a school that had a great academic reputation. The Big East had just been formed, but the ACC was the best conference in all of basketball.

That summer, I played on the Riverside Church AAU team with some great players. One of my teammates was Rodney McCray. He played at Mount Vernon HS and went on to the University of Louisville before a successful career in the NBA. I remember sitting next to Rodney on the bus one day. He was a big guy with a big reputation, but he was soft-spoken and someone who was easy to like.

Rodney asked, "Where are you thinking about going to school?"

I said, "I am thinking of attending UNC."

Rodney replied, "Do you think you can play there?"

I love it when people doubt me!

That September, all four schools made home visits. It was an exciting experience having these legendary coaches visiting our home to discuss their programs. Most of the coaches discussed how I would fit into their team, the opportunity to play, and the educational component.

UNC came in with Coach Dean Smith and Eddie Fogler. I recall Coach Smith being the most relaxed head coach to visit. My parents felt very comfortable with him. The one thing that stood out from that visit was the topic of playing time. The other programs gave me the impression that I would get to play right away. I was anxious to hear Coach Smith's thoughts. I distinctly remember him saying, "You would be lucky to play by the time you are a junior!" I leaned forward and said to myself, "I will show you!"

All four schools were great academic institutions. That was important to me and my family, as I knew basketball wouldn't last forever. I scheduled visits to Duke, UVA, UNC, and Notre Dame.

Planning for the campus visits, my mother took me shopping to buy me new clothes. We bought a nice tan wool blazer and a brown knit square bottom tie. I wore this on the Piedmont Airlines flight from LaGuardia Airport to Raleigh-Durham Airport for my first visit to Duke. When I landed, Duke Assistant Bob Wenzel was there to greet me. I remember how small the airport was. It seemed smaller than the Nassau Coliseum. We quickly arrived at baggage claim, and who do I see? UNC's Assistant Eddie Fogler! He was there picking up another recruit! It made me realize a few things real quick! One, the campuses of Duke and Carolina must be really close and two, no matter how special a program tried to make you feel in the recruiting process, you weren't the only one!

Duke had gone to the Final Four in 1978 with Jim Spanarkel, Mike Gminski, Gene Banks, Bob Bender, and Kenny Dennard. Spanarkel had just graduated, and I really liked his game. He was a 6-5 guard from Hudson Catholic in Jersey City, NJ. I even tried to shoot like him in high school, off the right side of the head. I could see playing like him. Gminski and Bender showed me around my first night. Mike had a sweet car. I believe it was a Camaro Z28. He was 6-11 and had the driver's seat mounted so it would go all the way back and touch the back seat! I sat behind Bob. We found a party on campus and drank a few Budweisers! I met the younger players. Chip Engelland and Tommy Emma were freshmen. Tommy was from Manhasset, NY, on Long Island, and was a prolific scorer in high school. Unfortunately, Tommy ended his life in June 2011. They were good guys, and we hung out late. The next morning, I was to meet with Head Coach Bill Foster. I must admit, I was a little "under the weather" after my late night, but I did have that nice jacket and tie on to try to impress Coach Foster!

The rest of the trip went well. Jim Peterson was the other recruit who joined me on the visit. Jim was 6-10 from Minnesota. We got along well. He ended up attending Minnesota and had a great NBA career. I still enjoy seeing Jim when our paths cross.

I recall the next weekend flying to Charlottesville to visit UVA. Terry Holland was their head coach. Jim Larranaga, currently the head coach at Miami, was the assistant who recruited me. He was from NYC and played at Molloy HS where my high school coach played. This made for an easy connection between the two of us. The campus was beautiful and they, too, had good players. Junior Jeff Lamp was an All-American and 7-4 sophomore Ralph Sampson may have been the most talented player in the country. Sophomore Jeff Jones took me around most of the weekend. Jeff, the current head coach at ODU, was easy to be with, as were the rest of the guys.

I believe the very next weekend I visited UNC. I fell in love with Carolina when Coach Smith led the USA team to the Gold Medal in the 1976 Olympics. Four Tar Heels were on that team—Mitch Kupchak, Tom LaGarde, Walter Davis, and Phil Ford. Then my love affair continued with the 1977 UNC team that went to the Final Four with freshman Mike O'Koren.

When I landed at the Raleigh-Durham Airport, UNC Assistant Eddie Fogler, a NYC native, was there to greet me. Again, I made the short trek to baggage claim, and lo and behold, there is Duke Assistant Bob Wenzel with another re-cruit! Gotta love the ACC!

UNC was on spring break, so there wasn't much happening on campus. However, practice had started. Back then, October 15 was always the first day of practice, so I got to see Coach Smith and the Tar Heels in action! What a treat. Mike O'Koren was now a senior. He was from Jersey City, NJ, and played in high school with Duke's Jim Spanarkel at Hudson Catholic. The way basketball is interwoven is eerie.

As I sat courtside, Coach Smith ran practice with precision. There was a practice plan that was timed to the minute. Players and coaches were moving from one drill to the next with an energy and intensity that was captivating. I took a notepad and started taking notes on the drills and terminology the coaches were using. The Carolina Blue practice uniforms with the players' names on the back were impressive. The hustle was amazing. I remember Dave Colescott diving headfirst for a loose ball like his life depended on it ... and this was practice! I loved every minute of it.

The only thing that gave me pause was the emblem on Coach Smith's shorts! It was a marijuana leaf! I was thinking, "What is Dean Smith doing with a logo of pot on his shorts?" Come to find out it was the emblem of a sportswear company that didn't have anything to do with pot!

We toured the campus and I met with a math professor. I loved math in high school. Sister John Rose taught calculus and was a great inspiration to me. I loved the fact that there was a problem with only one right answer. It fed into my competitive nature to solve the problem. In NY, we had the state Regents. After taking the final, I got home and was having lunch. The phone rang and it was for me. Sr. John Rose was on the line! I was nervous. This can't be good! She said, "Doherty, you idiot!" Right then, I knew I did well. Sr. John continued, "You forgot to check a radical!" I got a ninety-eight!

Mike O'Koren and I hung out in his room watching the UNC football team play at NC State. All we did was talk. I loved Mike. He was 6-7. I was 6-7. He was from New Jersey. I was from New York. I fell in love with his game when I saw him as a freshman score thirty-one points in the Final Four against UNLV. He was a helluva player, and now, I realized he was a helluva guy.

The rest of the weekend was low-key. I went to mass on campus with Long Islander Chris Brust and Coach Smith drove me around town in his Lincoln Continental. He had 8-track tapes in there and a lot of cigarette butts!

When I landed back at LaGuardia, my mother was there to greet me. She could see the excitement on my face, and said, "You're going to Carolina, aren't you?"

The next weekend, I was supposed to visit Notre Dame. An Irish Catholic kid from NY being recruited by Notre Dame was special! All the nuns at my high school wanted me to go there. The only reservation my parents had about me going to UNC was their fear I would stop going to mass!

Eddie Fogler told me that they were recruiting two wing players. Since 6-6 Al Wood and 6-4 Mike Pepper were seniors, they needed to fill that void. Coach Fogler said Clarke Bynum was going to visit the next weekend. I knew that Clarke was a 6-8 forward from SC and that we had similar games. We could play together, but I also viewed him as competition. I liked UNC enough that I told my parents I wanted to commit to play at UNC and I was going to cancel my visit to Notre Dame. If Clarke was going to come, I wanted him to know that I was going to be there first. I believe Clarke didn't end up visiting UNC, but he went on to be a worthy opponent at Clemson. He was a good player and a great guy. In 2000, he fought off a passenger who tried to hijack a plane with almost four hundred passengers. Heroic! Unfortunately, he passed away in 2007 from cancer.

By committing to UNC in October 1979, I was the earliest commitment Coach Smith had ever received. I chose Carolina because I believed they would have a chance to win the national title each year and I felt Dean Smith would appreciate what I would bring to the team. I knew what I wasn't! I wasn't a great athlete, but I was a savvy player who could help the team win. There were risks though. Would I get playing time at such a prestigious program? They bring in All-Americans every year. But, with Mike and Al being seniors my freshman year, I could only control what was in front of me, not who was coming in behind me.

Who would know that Michael Jordan would come to UNC the next year!

I was the sixth man my freshman year, getting significant playing time. It was awesome playing in the ACC, and interesting to play against Duke and UVA, the two other ACC schools that I visited. We made it to the 1981 Final Four, where we beat UVA. We faced Indiana in the finals, a team we beat in Chapel Hill in December. That afternoon, President Ronald Reagan got shot. We sat in the locker room in the Spectrum in Philadelphia wondering if we would play the game. After a long delay, we lost to the Hoosiers and their talented All-American Isiah Thomas.

The next year, we had the core of our team back—Jimmy Black, James Worthy, and Sam Perkins were all starters the year before. Then there was me and this skinny freshman from Wilmington, NC named "Mike" Jordan. We were ranked pre-season number one by *Sports Illustrated*, and they put the returning starters and me on the front cover with Coach Smith. No Mike Jordan! Coach wasn't going to put a freshman in that picture because he hadn't earned his spot yet!

I was sitting on "The Wall" in front of the undergraduate library watching the activity on campus when someone ran up to me, handed me a magazine, and said, "Have you seen the latest *Sports Illustrated*?" There I was! On the front cover of Sports Illustrated with my teammates and Coach Smith. It was surreal. I loved seeing that magazine each week. As a kid, I would idolize the athletes on the cover and now, here I was on the cover of SI!

That magical season ended with UNC winning the National Championship in New Orleans. It was Coach Smith's first after six trips to the Final Four, and I was a starter. The 1982 Final Four was loaded with talented players from Georgetown, Houston, and Rodney McCray's Louisville team!

"Yes, Rodney, I can play at UNC!"

CHAPTER FOUR:

HEARTBREAK

"The heart will break, but broken live on."
—Lord Byron

I started at UNC my last three years on teams that were always in the Top Ten of the country. We were good. We were elite. It was the epitome of college basketball. We had a tremendous coaching staff that included assistants Bill Guthridge, Eddie Fogler, and Roy Williams! Coach Smith would call it, "The Super Highway." We stayed in the best hotels, flew first class, signed autographs, and played in front of packed arenas. People treated us like rock stars.

After my last year, the seniors and any player going early to the NBA would meet with Coach Smith to discuss our futures. Most players finishing up at UNC expected to play professional basketball, either in the NBA or Europe. Coach Smith would talk to us about our prospects of playing professionally, and he would guide us in choosing an agent. I left those meetings feeling like I had a realistic chance of being a third-round pick in the NBA Draft and making a team.

I was invited to play in two NBA pre-draft events. One was the Portsmouth Invitational Tournament (PIT) and the other was the NBA Pre-Draft Camp in Chicago. My teammates Sam Perkins and Michael Jordan didn't attend those events because they were already considered top five NBA draft picks. Those of us who weren't elite college players were given the opportunity to improve our "stock" in front of NBA scouts.

At the PIT, I was on a team with Jerome Kersey. He was 6-7 from Division II Longwood College. I had never heard of him before, but he got my attention in the first workout. Jerome was very strong and athletic, and he played hard. His skills were limited, but his talent was evident. When the games began and the lineups were introduced, I received loud applause from the fans in attendance. With the event being in Virginia, there were a lot of ACC and Tar Heel fans there. When play started, it was like an organized pick-up game. Players were going one-on-one, taking poor shots and not getting back on defense. This was not the type of play I was accustomed to, but I tried to adapt. By doing so, I struggled, due to my lack of athletic ability. That night, doubt started to creep into my mind as I wondered if I was good enough for the NBA.

As the PIT went on, players I never heard of started to stand out. Kersey played very well, and there was this guard from a tiny school in the state of Washington. He was a small point guard from Gonzaga. I had never heard of Gonzaga and I had never heard of him. He went on to win the Most Outstanding Player Award for the whole event. His name was John Stockton.

Both Jerome Kersey and John Stockton went on to great NBA careers. Jerome was drafted in the second round of the

NBA Draft by the Portland Trail Blazers and won an NBA Championship with the San Antonio Spurs. He played sixteen years in the NBA, and suddenly passed away at the tender age of fifty-two. John was drafted in the first round by the Utah Jazz and played nineteen years for that organization. He played on the 1992 Olympics team and was inducted into the Naismith Hall of Fame.

After struggling in the PIT, I attended the Chicago Pre-Draft Camp. The athleticism was elite, as there were better players than at the PIT. My game continued to get exposed. I wasn't a good one-on-one player, as I struggled to guard quick players and couldn't get a good shot off against their quickness. I felt my stock continue to drop.

For some reason, I remained optimistic that I would still be drafted in the third round of the NBA Draft. There was a false sense of security, since I started at UNC for three years on some great teams.

The day was June 19, 1984. I was speaking at Campbell College's (now Campbell University) basketball camp. It was a large camp with about seven hundred campers there. The NBA Draft was that day, but only the top talent was invited to attend the draft in New York City. Before I was to speak, I called the UNC Basketball Office several times using a pay phone at the gym. Linda Woods, who was Coach Smith's long-time secretary, answered and I asked, "Any news?" There was no news of me being drafted. I remember calling her at least three times as the draft moved through the first few rounds. Then it was time for me to address the campers. I was frazzled as I got up in front of the kids. My mind was racing about the draft.

I finally got into a flow teaching the young players about the game I loved since I was a fourth grader. Then suddenly,

I felt a tap on my shoulder. It was the director of the camp, interrupting my talk. He whispered in my ear, "Sixth round. Cleveland." My knees started to buckle. Tears started to sting my eyes. "Sixth round! Cleveland!" I thought to myself! No one makes the NBA drafted that low, and the Cleveland Cavaliers were the worst team in basketball.

I did my best to compose myself and finish the lecture, but I was numb. After I was done, I drove back to my apartment in Chapel Hill. I thought about my future the whole ride home. What happened? Why doesn't the NBA think I am good enough?

To make matters worse, the next morning, my radio alarm clock went off. It was tuned to the local radio station. While still in bed, I heard the sports reporter listing the ACC players drafted by the NBA. He was going down the list and I heard, "UVA's Rick Carlisle third round Boston Celtics." I immediately started to cry in my bed. Rick and I had developed a good friendship that spring, meeting for workouts in Charlottesville and in Chapel Hill as we prepared for the draft. I would stay at his apartment and he would stay at mine. "Third round Boston Celtics" was where I wanted to be drafted! I loved Larry Bird, and I felt my style of play would be a fit there. Instead, I was drafted in the sixth round by Cleveland!

That summer, I ended up tweaking my back and missed rookie camp with the Cavs, but I was invited back for veteran's camp. I remember World B. Free was there and how big and athletic everyone was. Even the players who weren't considered good players were good. Former UNC player George Karl was the coach, and he ended up telling me that I wasn't going to make the team. I appreciated the fact that he drafted me, probably at the request of Coach Smith.

I went into a free fall emotionally. For twelve years, I loved basketball and it loved me back. It was like a marriage. We had great times together. We laughed. We cried. We won. We lost. We traveled together. We grew together. We were synonymous. Matt Doherty was a basketball player. That was my identity and I liked it. It felt good. I was proud of that identity. All I ever wanted to be was a basketball player. Now I was being told I wasn't good enough. My basketball career was over!

CHAPTER FIVE:

PLAN B

"Screw you, basketball!"

I felt betrayed by basketball. I had devoted my life to the game, and it turned its back on me! I didn't want to hang onto the game like many guys I saw. I wanted to move on.

I always had a backup plan. My backup plan was to work on Wall Street and make money. I had interned briefly at an investment firm in NYC one summer during college, and former UNC player Tommy Kearns was a successful Wall Street executive who had been helpful to me.

That fall, I moved back home to Long Island and started interviewing for jobs. I would take the Long Island Railroad from Hicksville into Penn Station each day. I ended up at Kidder Peabody. Former UNC football player Max Chapman was a key executive there and gave me the opportunity. Although I loved living in NYC, I hated my job. I would hit the snooze button each morning, dreading to go to work.

I recall the excitement of March Madness on Wall Street. All the traders and brokers took out NCAA Championship brackets and started trading teams. Just like they were stocks or bonds, NCAA Tournament teams were being bought and sold on "The Street." I was popular in March, as I was everyone's consultant on the trading floor!

There was one March where I recall various coaches leading their teams to the Final Four. I looked out the window and thought, "What do those coaches have on me? I played for arguably the best basketball coach in the world. My background was as good as the coaches in the NCAA Tournament. Maybe…?"

That summer, I became more restless with my career choice as a government bond salesman. The yield curve didn't excite me. The Federal Reserve Bank wasn't my go-to topic after work. I was doing the radio for St. Francis College in Brooklyn with Todd Ant. Bobby Valvano was the coach. I loved doing those games and the camaraderie that came with it. The closer I got to the game, the more I wanted to be in the huddle, not outside looking in.

I remember talking to Coach Smith about college coaching. He said, "If a job opened up in Montana, would you take it?" I hesitated. He was testing me. Maybe I didn't want to be a college coach?

A few months later, I had all I could stand. I had been there for four years. I realized that money didn't motivate me. I tapped my boss at Kidder Peabody on the shoulder and told him, "I'm leaving." He said, "When are you coming back?" He must have thought I was going to lunch. I told him I wanted to leave my job.

I ended up moving to Charlotte, thinking I would get into the real estate business. I thought Charlotte would become the next Atlanta in terms of growth. (I was right!) I moved there and got a part-time job with Sockwell & Anderson. It was a search firm that recruited banking executives. I enjoyed the position very much. Ed Sockwell had an AAU team that I ended up coaching. I was immediately bitten by the coaching bug. I would plan practice and organize the team. I would pick up players and drive them home. It was energizing.

During that time, I worked as a radio analyst for the Davidson College basketball team. That spring, Davidson made a coaching change and hired "Mr. McKillop" as their coach. Coach McKillop hired me as an assistant coach, and I never looked back!

I loved working with Bob and the staff. We worked long hours, but it didn't seem like work. It was my passion. I was making $25,000 and driving a used Ford Taurus. I made $25,000 the year before as a bonus working at Kidder!

Davidson struggled those first three years, but we were building something together. I loved the recruiting, the game planning, watching film, and working with the players.

While I was at Davidson, Roy Williams had just left UNC to become the head coach at Kansas. I was very close to Coach Williams as a player and stayed in touch with him. In the summer, I worked the summer camps at UNC and at Kansas. I wanted to stay connected to Coach Williams and Coach Smith, in the event that a job would open up on their staffs. The "UNC Family" was very tight and Coach Smith had a large network.

In 1992, after three years at Davidson, Coach Williams hired me to join him in Lawrence, Kansas. By that time, I had met and married Kelly. We ended up living there for seven great years. Our son, Tucker, was born there, and our teams had great success. My first year, we went to the 1993 Final

Four in New Orleans! We faced UNC in the semifinals. It was surreal to me. Just eleven years prior, I was playing for UNC in New Orleans where we won the Championship. Now I was an assistant coach for KU with Roy Williams going against Dean Smith and the mighty Tar Heels. UNC beat us in the semifinals and went on to win the Championship two nights later.

One incident illustrates my great love of coaching. When the Kansas Lottery was up to around fifty million dollars, my friends were discussing what they would do if they won the lottery. Most said that they would retire. When they asked me what I would do if I won the lottery, I said without hesitation, "I would still coach!"

CHAPTER SIX:

DEVELOPING A WINNING CULTURE

"Culture eats strategy for breakfast."
—Peter Drucker

It was April 1, 1999 when I was announced as the head coach of Notre Dame. Just eleven years prior, I quit my job on Wall Street! Amazing how I used to dream about coaching college basketball while sitting at my desk at 10 Hanover Square in lower Manhattan and now I am the head coach at the University of Notre Dame!

"Life is a series of decisions and dealing with the consequences. The better decisions you make, the better your life will be." I came up with this quote and have said it many times to young people. Whether it be decisions about careers or spouses or money, every decision has a consequence. Most decisions require risk. I made a decision to quit my job in NYC. I made a decision to move to Charlotte. I made a decision to work for Bob and Roy. I made a decision to marry Kelly. I made a decision to pass up other head coaching choices and wait for the right one. Notre Dame was the right one!

My family joined me in South Bend, IN, for the press conference. Kelly, pregnant with our daughter, Hattie, and my two-year-old son, Tucker, were there along with my parents. I flew my parents in from New York for this tremendously exciting day. My mother's parents were Irish immigrants who raised their family in the Bronx. We all toured the beautiful campus that afternoon. It was a special day for this Irish Catholic kid from Long Island. As we approached the Basilica on campus, my mother grabbed my arm and said, in all seriousness, "Matthew, if you couldn't be a Catholic priest, being the head coach at Notre Dame is a close second!" You gotta love mothers!

Before we arrived in South Bend, I had already hired long-time friend Doug Wojcik to join my staff. He was an assistant at the Naval Academy where he starred alongside David Robinson on their 1986 Elite Eight team. Doug was one of the hardest workers I knew in the industry. We recruited the same types of players when I was at Davidson—good players who were tough, with a good academic profile and high character. Doug and his wife, Lael, joined us for the press conference. He and I were determined to set the tone for the future of Notre Dame basketball.

I decided to take my time adding to the rest of the staff. I believe that it is critical to hire people who are a good fit, and I wanted to go slowly with this process. I always felt it was easy to hire, but hard to fire. The future of your program and the welfare of your family are put in the hands of the people you ask to join your staff. This process cannot be taken lightly.

The other thing with adding to your staff is augmentation. I knew what I was good at and what I liked. I enjoyed recruiting, coaching, and raising money. It was important for me to have people on my staff with an array of skills so that we would complement each other and not duplicate each other.

The next order of business was to tour the facilities. Since I took the job before seeing the campus, I was anxious to see what may lie ahead. My first time seeing the locker room, I was shocked! It was like a high school locker room. What I saw didn't represent the overall excellence of the University. The culture at Notre Dame was centered around football, and the basketball facilities were in disrepair. The feeling I got was that "If the locker room was good enough for Adrian Dantley (legendary player in the 1970s), it should be good enough for our players!"

Meeting with the players was critical. I wanted to get in front of them one-on-one as soon as possible. I wanted to connect with them. I wanted to hear their concerns and how we can improve THEIR program. One of my early meetings was with returning star Troy Murphy. Troy was the Big East Freshman of the Year. I remember asking one critical question, "What would you like to see improved in the program?"

Troy mentioned two things. Number one, he wanted access to the practice facility. "The Pit" was a small gym that was attached to the arena. The arena was used for different events, so he couldn't gain access to the main floor all the time. "The Pit" was closed when there wasn't a scheduled practice, so the only place Troy could work out was the student wellness center. This meant he was trying to get shots up when other students were playing pick-up. This was not conducive to a star player trying to improve his game. Number two, he asked that the cheerleaders be ready and in place when the team came out onto the court for warm-ups before the game! I couldn't believe what I was hearing. That was the definite sign of apathy in the basketball program.

My goal that day was to get Troy a key to "The Pit" by the time I got on my flight that evening to go recruiting. I worked the phones and talked to the head of facilities, determined to get Troy and his teammates access to "The Pit." It was paramount that I send a signal to the team that I was committed to them. As I was boarding the plane, I finally was able to secure the key for Troy. I called him and said, "I got you a key to 'The Pit'!"

The rest of April was a blur as I met with players, academic support, and the director of admissions. In addition, I scheduled meetings with senior vice president Father Bill Beauchamp and athletic director Mike Wadsworth. My goal was to ask them for a new locker room! We needed to show our players and recruits that Notre Dame was committed to having a first-class basketball program. On top of that, I wanted construction of the locker room to start by October! This was a big ask for a first-year head coach, especially after accepting the job. Usually, you negotiate these things before you take a job, but I never was able to see how bad the locker room was before my first day on campus. Father Bill and Mike agreed that we needed the locker room and we quickly raised one million dollars to start the work!

Asking for the money and the commitment to building a new locker room was huge for our program. The key to getting this done was the approachability and the respect I felt for both Father Bill and Mike. I made the ask with facts due to my knowledge of the industry. Having worked at Kansas and recruiting against the top programs in the country, I knew what other programs had. But I understood Notre Dame. We didn't need the "Taj Mahal" of locker rooms because the players we were going to recruit were coming to Notre Dame for more than facilities. They were interested in a great education from a world-class institution with an alumni network that could set them up for life. The key was we needed a locker room that wouldn't scare away a prospect. Construction began, and by the start of practice, we ended up with a first-class locker room!

We continued to make changes to the physical appearance of the office and "The Pit" to make it more attractive to recruits and to create pride within the program. Doug Wojcik had an ugly tree cut down outside our office and cleaned up an area that would flood the sidewalk. My wife helped spruce up my office. We had an iconic picture put in my office of Dwight Clay's jumper that ended UCLA's eighty-eight-game winning streak. You could taste the momentum growing within the program!

When you take over a program, former employees will often offer their advice. You have to take this with a grain of salt. Often, they're trying to create goodwill so you would either keep them on staff or recommend them for another job. There were two comments made that stuck with me. Number one, senior "Jimmy Dillon wasn't an effective player and he was a distraction. He wasn't a great student and often got into trouble." Number two, "The receptionist was not very effective and you should consider replacing her."

I firmly believe that it's important to give everyone a "clean slate." I don't want to use the bias of a former staff member to impact decisions I was going to make about personnel. I know I wouldn't want to be viewed that way if I was a player or an employee with new leadership taking over. I would hope that a new leader would give me the opportunity for a fresh start.

We had tough workouts to push the players. I wanted to bring back the pride of Irish basketball. I remember Notre Dame basketball as a kid growing up on Long Island, watching them beat John Wooden's UCLA team and the fans storming the court. I loved Notre Dame. Kelly Tripucka was one of my favorite players. I wore number forty-four in college, partly because that was Kelly's number at ND. I wanted to bring those glory days back to South Bend!

I finally completed my staff. I believed everyone's skill set complemented each other and together we could make a big impact on Notre Dame basketball. One of the things I learned from Roy Williams in hiring a staff was that you should hire people you know well. If are you looking to hire somebody you don't know, someone you know well needs to know that person well. This process ensures you know what you are getting in a staff member.

I hired Bob McKinnon, Fred Quartlebaum, and David Cason. I knew Bob since he worked UNC's camp when I was a player. Doug worked with Fred at Navy and David played for my good friend Kevin Stallings at Illinois State. This gave me great comfort in adding them to my team!

In addition, associate athletic director Bubba Cunningham oversaw men's basketball. Bubba, now the athletic director at UNC, was a great administrator and we quickly became fast friends. I also inherited a great strength and conditioning coach named Tony Rolinski and longtime trainer Skip Meyer. Tony was awesome as he laid the foundation of toughness and grit through his work in the weight room. Tony bought into the culture I wanted to create and pushed the players out of their comfort zones. Skip ended up being a valuable member of the staff as he would have the pulse of the team. This feedback was invaluable as he would tell me in confidence how the players were feeling. Then I could "push the right buttons" to make sure they were ready to compete.

After several months, I ended up making a change with my administrative assistant. My personal assistant had been there a while and I felt she grew complacent. I wanted some new energy, so I asked her to leave. I learned that it was important to give her a chance, but when I felt the need to make the change, it was important to do it quickly and professionally. If you let a decision like this linger and avoid crucial conversations, no one wins. It creates an environment of apathy. I talked with Bubba and then we talked with human resources. I think it's important to handle things the right way. The person from HR and I met with my assistant and had the crucial conversation. This was my first time ever asking someone to leave, and it wasn't easy, but I think it's important for the whole organization that you have everybody working together with the same passion and vision for a common cause. One person can make all the difference in the world.

I ended up hiring Stephanie Reed to be my executive assistant. She had recently graduated from Notre Dame, so she knew the school as well as anyone and she loved basketball. I felt this would be a huge asset. I didn't want to go the traditional route and hire from the pool of assistants available on campus. I wanted to try to avoid the politics and bring in somebody fresh who would be 100 percent loyal to me. Stephanie ended up being a great hire, and was Mike Brey's longtime assistant before she left to relocate to another part of the country.

Finally, we moved into our new locker room. The players were filled with excitement. It was first class. In the team room, I had pictures put up of all the All-Americans who had worn the Irish jersey. There were a lot of them! We practiced for several weeks. The workouts were intense and productive. The players were emotionally invested, as was my staff. We ended the pre-season by playing an exhibition game against Marathon Oil and lost by twenty-four points. MARATHON OIL! Ohio State had already played them and won by twenty-five points. We were scheduled to play at Ohio State in our first regular season game the next week! The day after that loss, there was an article in the *South Bend Tribune* entitled "Lackadaisical Effort Dooms the Irish." As I read the headline, I started to steam. I thought, "I have been called a lot of things, but 'lackadaisical' wasn't one of them." We were scheduled to have that day off, but I met with my staff and told them to call the players and have them in the gym for practice, but there would be no basketballs!

Growing up on Long Island, playing at Prospect Park, and having played for Bob McKillop at Holy Trinity HS taught me how to compete and fight for everything on the court. It was a form of respect. Respect was earned. If you backed down, you were viewed as weak. Plus, working for Roy Williams at Kansas, it was the same way. Bob and Roy were both intense competitors and didn't accept anything less than 100 percent. As a result, I was wired this way, too.

On the baseline! We ran and ran and ran. I yelled at them before one sprint, "I got you a new locker room and you give me that type of effort! On the baseline!"

After about thirty minutes of running, Matt Carroll, who was a good freshman who had a nice NBA career, raised his hand. He asked with a desperate look, "Coach, can we get some water?" I said, "You know, Matt, I am getting parched blowing this whistle." Then I signaled to a manager to bring me a cup of water. I slowly drank the cup of water right in front of the team. When I was done, I said, "On the baseline!"

I was being a hard-ass, but I wanted to make a point that lack of effort will never be accepted at Notre Dame. When I got the job, the program had a reputation of being "soft." I was determined to turn it into a hard-nosed program. I don't care if we lose, but we will play hard!

We continued to run. Some players "fell out," not be able to run anymore. I told those players to get out of the gym. Several players continued to run. All-American Troy Murphy and Oklahoma transfer Ryan Humphrey hung tough. Finally, after about an hour of running hard, I ended the workout. I walked out of the gym. I didn't want to see them. I didn't want any small talk. I was still mad!

Years later, Assistant Bob MacKinnon said it was like the scene from the movie *Miracle on Ice* where actor Kurt Russell played Coach Herb Brooks. Coach Brooks had the team skate as punishment after the USA hockey team lost an exhibition game. The team skated until they broke down, realizing that they needed to play as a team for each other and for the United States of America. That team ended up beating a dominant Soviet team on their way to winning the 1980 Gold Medal!

We had a few more days of practice in preparation for our game at number five-ranked Ohio State. My players were mad at me and I was still mad at them. There was no small talk between us that week.

We traveled to Columbus, OH, in a bus. Game day shoot-around went well. At the end of the workout, I rolled a ball on the floor and dove on it, ripping my warmup pants. I wanted the team to know that every loose ball was going to be ours.

Pre-game meal at Notre Dame always ended with Mass. A priest traveled with us. I was nervous about how Mass and a priest sitting on our bench would feel to me and the team. Not everyone was Catholic, and I didn't know how I would act on the bench or in the locker room. Would having a priest in my locker room and my huddles be a distraction?

At the end of Mass, the priest handed out Medals of different Saints. As the priest was ready to hand out the Medals, he said, "This is a Medal of St. Jude, the patron Saint of lost causes!"

"What?" I said to myself! Lost causes! Come on, Father!

The Buckeyes were coming off a Final Four appearance. They were a talented team. It was a close game throughout. We played with poise and confidence. We ended up beating them on a last-second shot by David Graves! Harold Swanigan set a heckuva pick to free David for the jump shot!

The coaches' wives made the trip to Columbus and sat behind the bench. My wife, Kelly, brought our two children, Hattie and Tucker. I went over and picked up my son and went over to be interviewed by ESPN's Bill Raftery after the game! After handing Tucker back to Kelly, I ran toward the locker room. I will never forget the look on the players' faces as they greeted me in the hallway. Jumping up and down, we embraced!

That is one of the reasons you coach. Pushing players out of their comfort zones to achieve success they couldn't have imagined!

The bus ride home was magical. Smiles across everyone's faces. Phone calls of congratulations from friends. When we arrived back at South Bend, we unloaded our bags in the locker room. One of the players wrote "304" on the whiteboard. That was the number of sprints they ran in that hard workout just a few days before. Several players would write "304" on their sneakers the rest of the year! They were invested!

The good thing about basketball is that you play a lot of games. The bad thing about basketball is you play a lot of games. We couldn't enjoy the Ohio State win too long, as Siena was coming to South Bend to play us a few nights later in the Pre-Season NIT. They were a scrappy team coached by Paul Hewitt. We needed to get ready! The game was scheduled for a Thursday night.

As we were planning for our first home game, there was great excitement, but I learned that the band wasn't going to be able to attend! What? No band for our opening game? We had a home football game on Saturday and the marching band practiced on Thursday nights. I was hot! This was a true sign that basketball wasn't important at Notre Dame. I had no problem being "second fiddle" to the legendary football program, but I didn't want to be disrespected. I talked to Bubba about it and I was told that the band isn't under the control of the athletic department. I was on my own. I called the band director and told him he must have about three hundred band members and could he send over about thirty of them to perform at the game. He said he might be able to get some band members to our game by halftime! I pounded my fist hard on my desk and said, "If you don't get the band to our game BEFORE tipoff, I don't want them to show up at all." Imagine the pep band rolling into the Joyce Center at halftime? What signal does that give our players and fans?

The pep band showed up before tipoff. We beat Siena! On to NYC for the Pre-Season NIT semifinals in Madison Square Garden!

We had some great wins that season. Our first Big East game was at highly ranked UConn. They had just come off a National Championship and were led by Jim Calhoun. We prepared for their press. I had scouted UConn the two times we played them at Kansas, and we won both games. We handled their press to perfection, often leading to good shots. I remember going into halftime, and freshman sharpshooter Matt Carroll was 0-5. I looked at Matty in front of the team and told him, "You're the best shooter in the game. When you are open, knock it down!" Matty ended up going 5-5 in the second half. We didn't turn the ball over against the press, and we showed great physical and mental toughness by going on the road to beat UConn for our first Big East win.

Before we played our last regular season game at Georgetown, I was standing in the hallway ready to address the team in the locker room. I asked Skip, "How are the guys?" He said, "They are scared!" Shocked, I asked, "Why?" He said, "They were always intimidated by Georgetown!" I ripped up my pre-game notes and stormed into the locker room. I lit into the players, challenging them to be the aggressor. "What is the worst thing that can happen? You might get a bloody nose! What are you afraid of? They put their uniforms on just like you do!" I told them, "When you set picks on them, I want to hear the air come out of their lungs!" We proceeded to go out and kick their butts! It was never close! I remember sitting in the Reagan Washington Airport after that game on a beautiful sunny day, waiting to board our plane back home with one of the most satisfying feelings I ever had. If I didn't communicate with Skip before the game, we probably would have lost!

You have to mine for the truth!

We played the Big East Tournament in Madison Square Garden. Notre Dame had never won a Big East Tournament game to that point. In the first round, we were facing a scrappy Rutgers team who we lost to on the road during the regular season. While sitting courtside doing the pre-game radio show about an hour and a half before tipoff, the maintenance staff was adjusting one of the baskets and the Rutgers players were shooting at the other. Our guys were dribbling while the basket was being adjusted. Then the maintenance staff went to fix the other goal. I noticed the Rutgers players change sides and shot on the goal that had just been adjusted, AND MY PLAYERS JUST CONTINUED TO DRIBBLE ON THE SIDELINE!

During the season, I remember getting mad at the team for their soft play and asked them, "Who on this team has a glass backboard in their driveway?" About three quarters of the team raised their hands. I said, "That is the problem with this team! We are soft!"

When it was time for the pre-game talk, I lit into the team, telling them, "We got punked by Rutgers and the game hadn't even started yet! How do we stand there and let those guys take our basket! What are we afraid of?"

We proceeded to go out and "punk" Rutgers, winning the first Big East Tournament game in Notre Dame history. Pretty cool!

We ended up facing Leonard Hamilton's Miami team the next night. They were talented and tough. We had lost to them twice during the regular season. The game came down to the wire. We were down two points with a few seconds to go and I called time-out to set up a play. As we were in the huddle, I could hear the crowd starting to chant, "Let's go, Irish!" I told the team to listen. Notre Dame fans were everywhere, especially in New York City.

We ran a play for Troy Murphy. David Graves set a great pick for Troy to get an open three-pointer. The shot came up short. We lost, but we fought, and I was proud of them!

Now we had to travel back to South Bend and wait. We had to wait to see if the NCAA Selection Committee would call our name to be a part of March Madness. We set up some food in our beautiful team room for the players and staff to watch the Selection Show. The brackets were being announced as we sat in anticipation of hearing Notre Dame being selected. One bracket. No Irish. The second bracket. No Irish. The third bracket. No Irish! I thought we had a good chance to hear our team called, but as a leader, I had to brace for our team not being called. I felt it critical that I be prepared for the worst. The final bracket was called. No Irish!

I quickly gathered the team and staff into the adjacent locker room. As I walked in, I gained my composure and said, "We are all disappointed that we didn't make the NCAA Tournament. The only thing we can do now is win the NIT and show the Committee we deserved to make the NCAA Tournament. The worst thing we can do is feel sorry for ourselves and lay an egg in the NIT."

Our players responded. We beat BYU and Michigan at home and went on to Madison Square Garden, again, for the NIT semifinals! Madison Square Garden became our second home. We played great against a good Penn State team and faced Wake Forest in the finals. We ended up losing to Wake, but we had a terrific season. We all felt the foundation had been laid for success. Great things were on the horizon for Notre Dame basketball!

Ironically, the last team to make the NCAA Tournament field was UNC! They had struggled during the season until football great Julius Peppers joined the team after the football season was over. Carolina got hot at the right time and made it all the way to the Final Four!

We beat five ranked teams that year, three of them on the road! Who said Notre Dame basketball was soft!

By the way, Jimmy Dillon, the kid I was told was a problem, ended up being one of the best leaders I have ever been around. He would take our team on early morning runs in the pre-season and then they would gather for team breakfast. He ended up with single season records in steals and assists! Jimmy was a savvy guy with a great personality who elevated the play of the team. In addition, Karen Wesolek, the receptionist, ended up being one of the best workers I've ever had. The more work we gave her, the more energized she became. They both just needed to be given an opportunity, some direction, and people who believed in them.

What a shame it would've been if I listened to the biased views of others and overlooked Jimmy and Karen! They ended up being two shining stars in what turned out to be a magical season.

CHAPTER SEVEN:

THE DECISION

"Always go with the choice that scares you most,
because that's the one that is going to help you grow."
—CAROLINE MYSS

I thought I would be in South Bend forever. We had a great season. Recruiting was going well. We received a big-time commitment from high school point guard Chris Thomas from Indiana. Notre Dame hadn't gotten the best players in the state with Bobby Knight at IU and Gene Keady at Purdue. We were making a lot of noise in the world of college basketball!

I remember playing golf at the Warren Golf Course at Notre Dame with some coaches who were in for our basketball camp. It was the most relaxed I had been since taking the job. My family was finally settled. We had a good season. We had a good team coming back and good recruits in the pipeline. Then I noticed there was a call I missed on my cell phone. I hate being on the phone while playing golf, but as a college coach, it is pretty much the norm. I checked the voice mail and listened to the message. UNC's Bill Guthridge just announced his retirement! My mind started to race. I shanked my next shot! Who retires in June? Coaches may leave college for the NBA at that time, but most college coaches retire right after the season. This seemed odd. Shank! Is his health okay? Shank! I was sure Coach Williams would take over at UNC. Shank! Will Kansas contact me when Roy leaves? Shank!

Everyone in the country believed Roy Williams would replace Coach Guthridge as the next coach at UNC, including me. I had been at Kansas with Coach Williams for seven years. We often talked privately about other coaching jobs. He had been mentioned about UCLA at least once, and other programs had approached him. He had been mentioned about a few NBA jobs, but he knew UNC was the best job in the country and believed it would be the only job he would ever leave KU for.

Kansas basketball was special. One could argue it was more special than UNC. It had a deep tradition. Dean Smith played there, and James Naismith, the man who invented the game of basketball, was its first coach. Wilt Chamberlain played there. Allen Fieldhouse was the loudest arena in the country. The home court advantage was huge. But Carolina was Carolina. The UNC brand was huge. The color was a brand. Michael Jordan played there. Roy had a beach house in SC. He loved to golf. Pinehurst No. 2 was sixty minutes from Chapel Hill. He was an assistant at UNC for Dean Smith for ten years. He and his wife were from NC. He attended UNC. His two children attended UNC. He and Coach Smith were very close. Even though he had been at KU for twelve seasons and had massive success with good young players in the program, many that I helped recruit, Carolina was home. It was a perfect fit for Roy Williams, and everyone knew it.

My family and I finally had a chance to get away on a vacation late June. We traveled to Lake Michigan and stayed at a cabin with Fred and Christy Quartlebaum. It was anything but a vacation. Bill Guthridge had just announced his retirement. Roy was expected to take the job. The KU job would be open and July recruiting was getting ready to start!

The cell service at the cabin stunk!

I called Dean Smith, seeking his advice in case Kansas were to call me about becoming the next Jayhawk coach. I remember Coach Smith saying, "It's not a done deal with Roy yet, and you are on the short list." A tremendous feeling of pride overcame me. Here is Dean Smith telling me I was on the list of candidates for the coaching vacancy at UNC!

I jokingly responded, "Well, that's a no-brainer."

After about seven long days of deliberation, Roy Williams finally decided to stay at Kansas. About a week later, I was flying on a private plane to Chapel Hill with Kelly to interview with Coach Smith and Athletic Director Dick Baddour about being the next head coach at UNC!

We stayed at the luxurious Siena Hotel. As I was getting out of the car, I saw a guy literally pop out from behind a bush and ask me if I was going to be the next coach at North Carolina! Think basketball is important in Chapel Hill!

Notre Dame AD Kevin White called me that night. He was a great AD to work for. Even though he joined ND after I was hired, we connected quickly. Kevin was now recruiting me to stay in South Bend, and we discussed a large contract extension.

As I prepared for my meeting with Coach Smith and Dick Baddour, I wanted clarity on three things:

1. Could I bring my staff with me from Notre Dame?

2. That this was going to be a rebuilding process after year one.

3. Would I be able to truly run the program as the head coach in the presence of Dean Smith?

If I felt comfortable that those three items would be clearly understood by all parties, then I would be able to take the head coaching position at UNC.

In talking with Dick, I emphasized my desire to bring my staff with me from Notre Dame. Doug Wojcik, Bob MacKinnon, Fred Quartlebaum, and David Cason were terrific assistants, great people, and wonderful friends. I couldn't leave them behind, especially in the middle of July. They would have a hard time finding another job. Plus, one of the many lessons I learned from Dean Smith was loyalty. The big issue was that my assistants would be replacing a staff of former UNC players who included Phil Ford, Dave Hanners, and Pat Sullivan. Phil may still be the most popular player in the history of Carolina basketball! All three were loyal Tar Heels who did a good job for Bill Guthridge and Dean Smith.

Dick agreed that I could bring my staff with me to Chapel Hill, and I didn't feel any pushback.

Check!

In addition, I recall telling Dick, "Our first year, we will be good. The second year, we won't, and our third year, we will be rebuilding." I then asked, "Are you tough enough to get through that with me?" He said, "Yes."

Check!

Finally, I was to meet with Coach Smith in the building that bears his name, the Dean E. Smith Center. I am going to meet with the man who I played for and revered. The man who won the most college basketball games up to that point.

The man who was ranked as the most popular figure in the State of North Carolina, along with Billy Graham and Andy Griffith!

Dean Smith was an icon, and I was going to meet with him in his building to discuss taking over his program. Even when I was a player, I was nervous talking with Coach. He was intimidating. You always wondered what he was thinking, and you always wanted to please him.

Many people were telling me that I should stay at Notre Dame because it was "my program" and that at UNC, it was still "Coach Smith's program." ESPN's Dick Vitale called me several times trying to convince me to stay at Notre Dame. Dick loved Notre Dame, but I was anxious to hear Coach Smith communicate his vision for the future. During our meeting, we discussed several topics. He asked me if I used a practice plan at Notre Dame. I loved talking basketball with him. He was a basketball savant, and I was eager to learn and ask questions. Finally, he offered the words I needed to hear, "It will be your program, and you can run it how you see fit."

Check!

We continued to discuss UNC and the philosophies of running a program, and he finally asked, "Well, can you take the job?" I responded, "I have to talk to my wife." Coach Smith replied, "Well, just a few weeks ago, you said it was a no-brainer." Typical Coach Smith!

My wife, Kelly, and I flew back to Notre Dame on a private plane. I remember saying to her, "I could be the head coach at North Carolina or I could be the head coach at Notre Dame!" Wow! How about that? It was both a blessing and a burden. Great options often lead to tough decisions!

The next few days were a blur. The Nike All-American Camp was taking place in Indianapolis, and I was there wearing my Notre Dame polo shirt, evaluating the high school talent. Chris Thomas was playing, and he had already committed to us at Notre Dame. He was a great talent who would complement the returning players we had in the program. Every coach in the country was present, and I felt a lot of eyes on me, as the world of college basketball was wondering if I would be the next coach at North Carolina.

I asked Roy Williams to meet with me to discuss my decision. He was my most trusted advisor on all the career decisions I made over the last eight years. We met in the lobby of the Marriott Hotel. Coaches were coming in and out. It was hectic. I was trying to focus on our conversation. It seemed rushed. The last thing I remember him saying was, "You can do that job!" Then we went our separate ways.

I was strongly leaning toward staying at Notre Dame. I loved the university and the players. Kevin White and I were becoming close, and I loved working with Bubba Cunningham. Kevin and I were both from Long Island, and he had a great reputation as a leader. He had already brought a new energy to the athletic department. In addition, I knew we were going to be good, as the foundation had been laid.

I could tell my staff had some trepidation on making the move to UNC. They had finally settled into South Bend and the university community. Everyone was in new homes and we all had young children. We were welcomed there, we had success, and the future was bright.

Coach Smith was a masterful recruiter, and he knew me probably better than I knew myself at that time. He knew what buttons to push. He had Michael Jordan call me. As Michael and I talked, I recall him finally saying, "If you don't take the job, Coach Smith will probably go outside the family and hire Rick Majerus." Button pushed! I knew right then that I would take the UNC job! I didn't want anyone outside "The Family" leading the program I loved so much. I felt no one but a former UNC player or coach would understand what it meant to be a part of the Carolina program.

Kevin White offered me a ten-year contract worth over twelve million dollars, along with a large signing bonus, to stay at Notre Dame. I remember the conversation as I was standing in my hotel room in Indianapolis. I was extremely flattered and humbled. I now knew what the market value was for me as a coach. I did have a brief thought that if that was the market value for me, why didn't I get that offer after the season? If that would have been offered, I would have gladly signed it and had been locked up at Notre Dame for a long time.

It would be very difficult for me to tell the players and recruits I was leaving. I remember visiting with transfer Ryan Humphrey in my office. We talked openly about the UNC opportunity that lay before me. Ryan was a high school All-American who we recruited at Kansas. He chose to play at Oklahoma, but decided to transfer after his first year, and I was grateful that he and his twin sister, Robyn, decided to attend Notre Dame. Ryan was the first transfer Notre Dame ever took. I took some minor grief from some alumni that I would "ruin the program" by bringing in transfers. Not only did Ryan flourish on the court at Notre Dame under Mike Brey, but he now is an assistant coach on Mike's staff! So much for ruining the program. Mike ended up bringing in several transfers who helped his program, and he once thanked me for "breaking the ice."

As my conversation with Ryan was winding down, he said to me, "You know, Coach. You are my friend first and my coach second. If you feel going to Carolina is the right thing,

I support you!" Oh my God! What maturity for a young man to say that to me, given the circumstances. To this day, Ryan and I remain close.

After much thought and sleepless nights, my wife and I decided to return to North Carolina. It was the state she grew up in, it was the program I loved, and it was the place we wanted to live. I didn't want to look back with regret that I didn't take the job. Plus, we would have a chance EVERY year to win the National Championship.

The hardest part was telling my players and Kevin that I was leaving. I wanted to tell the players in person. We met on campus to meet in a large room away from the Joyce Center. I got up in front of the players and tried to talk, but no words came out. I got emotional. It was one of the hardest things I ever had to do. I loved those guys. I loved that team and I love Notre Dame to this day!

CHAPTER EIGHT:

THE FIRST NINETY DAYS

"The first 90 days of a new role can determine your success or failure and have implications for the rest of your career. Initial impressions are crucial since perceptions are formed quickly and, although they may be based on limited information, once formed they typically stick."
— UNKNOWN

July 11, 2000 was the press conference to announce my hiring as the new head coach at the University of North Carolina. It was a big day. New blood in the Smith Center. Former Tar Heel champion returns home to lead the program. My staff and family were at the press conference, along with many friends. The large room was filled with media and athletic department staff. It was a proud day for Kelly and me. However, it was a difficult day for many others, as there was going to be significant change to a program that had not seen significant change for almost forty years. Dean Smith was the head coach at UNC for thirty-six years, and his long-time assistant, Bill Guthridge, took over the head coaching position for the following three years and retained the same assistant coaches. The secretarial staff of four had been in place for much of that time, too.

There was no time to celebrate. That night, my staff and I manned the phones, calling all the top recruits on our list. We knew that it would impress a recruit if they got a call from us the night of the press conference. We were on the phone past midnight, as we always worked from east coast to west coast, due to the time zones. We secured our first commitment in Jackie Manuel from Florida. We were recruiting him at Notre Dame, so we already had a good relationship, and I knew he was talented enough to help us win.

I finally got back to the luxurious suite on campus Dick Baddour secured for me and my family. As I walked into the room, it must have been 2 a.m. Who did I see waiting for me? Bobby Ellington. Bobby was my college roommate and one of my best friends. Here was a man who lived over an hour away in Greensboro, NC, waiting on his friend to share in this special moment. I love Bobby Ellington and am truly blessed that he is in my life.

My first day on the job, I hit the road to recruit, as I knew that recruiting was the lifeblood of any program. We had a lot of ground to make up. My first order of business was to see star recruit Carmelo Anthony in Baltimore. I had a private plane fly me to BWI Airport, and when I arrived at the small private plane terminal, I saw the *USA Today* newspaper, and my picture was in the upper right-hand corner on the front page! Carolina Basketball is national news!

Before I hit the road recruiting, I told Doug Wojcik to clean up the office. There were dead plants and stained carpet in the lobby. I was surprised to see how worn the offices looked. Old wooden trophies were on the wall from when I played, and there were no pictures of Michael Jordan in the lobby! I see everything through the eyes of prospects, and I felt the office and locker room needed a serious facelift! Doug did a magnificent job, as he did when we took over at Notre Dame. He quickly dressed up the lobby. We ended up renovating the locker room, created a new weight room, and updated our offices to look like a facility that North Carolina basketball deserved.

I asked Doug to put up a picture of Michael in the lobby. I wanted the iconic picture of Michael hitting the game winning shot against Georgetown in the 1982 National Championship game. There were two versions of that picture. One with our bench in the background and another with me in the back-ground standing at the free throw line as Michael was taking "The Shot." I wanted that picture placed in the lobby, so re-cruits could see that I played with the greatest player of all time.

The rest of July was a blur, as I was out every day evaluat-ing the talent and shadowing the top prospects on our list. We had focused on Jawad Williams from St. Edward HS in Cleveland, OH. He was a long athlete with a good perimeter jump shot. I shadowed him much of the summer. Maryland was recruiting him hard, too. Terp Assistant Coach Dave Dickerson spent a lot of time following Jawad, but not Head Coach Gary Williams. I made it a point to see Jawad as much as possible. When the July recruiting period was over, I sent Jawad a handwritten note every day, and I was the only coach on our staff who would call him. He was an "A-list" recruit for us, and I wanted him to feel special. There was one phone con-versation we had where I asked him what other schools he was considering. Jawad said, "Maryland." I could feel my adren-aline kick in. As I calmed myself, I said, "How many games did Gary Williams see you play in July?" I knew the answer wasn't many. I told Jawad how many times I saw him play. Then I asked, "What Maryland coach calls you each week?" I knew the answer. I told Jawad, "I saw you play more than Gary Williams. I call you every week, not one of my assistants, and I write you a handwritten note every day. What does that tell you?" Jawad said, "You want me more." I said, "Yes, I want you more. Every coach is somewhere in July, and I spent most of my time with you!" That was one of Roy's go-to lines in recruiting!

August came, and we had planned a family vacation to South Carolina. Roy Williams was kind enough to lend us his beach house. It wasn't much of a vacation for me, as I had film to watch and recruits to call. I remember bringing VHS tapes of UNC games from the past year. Two tapes I made sure I brought were the two Duke games. I studied them relentlessly. I noticed how Duke attacked the "point zone" defense by putting shooters in both corners, forcing Carolina's power forward to cover the whole baseline. I also remember former UNC great Brad Daugherty broadcasting the game. At one point late in the contest, he made a comment about how UNC was embarrassed by Duke. I made sure we used that clip in preparation for our first matchup against the Blue Devils!

While on "vacation," I received a call from the head of admissions at UNC. He told me some shocking news! Incoming All-American Jason Parker from Charlotte was being denied admission! What! School was starting in a few weeks! We were counting on the talented big man to add depth to the frontline and hopefully have a great career. I was told they flagged his SAT exam because the score jumped too high the last time he took it, and as a result, he wasn't an NCAA qualifier.

Some vacation!

When we returned to Chapel Hill, Coach Guthridge and I met in Charlotte to tell Jason and his family he was not going to be allowed to attend school! Jason didn't attend the visit, as I am sure he didn't want to stand the embarrassment, but we talked to his parents. It was a humbling experience, to say the least. I felt awful for Jason and his parents. I greatly appreciated Coach Guthridge's class in going along with me on that difficult trip.

Three days later, I learned that Kentucky and Wake Forest were now recruiting Jason Parker! How could that be? It turns out that Jason was in fact eligible because he took an honors class his freshmen year of high school that wasn't factored into his core GPA that UNC had calculated. He didn't need to take the SAT as many times as he did, and he, in fact, was an NCAA qualifier with the lower test score. Jason ended up committing to Kentucky, and they were on our schedule the next two years! If that had happened with my staff, someone would have been held accountable!

While all this was going on, the coaches and our families were living in apartments. We all had young children, and we were all trying to sell houses in South Bend and buy new houses in Chapel Hill. Two of the coaches' wives were pregnant. God bless coaches' wives!

We ended up buying a nice home on a golf course that I thought we would be in forever, but it needed work. Kelly acted as a general contractor ... two years in a row! We did the same thing in South Bend. Tucker was barely two years old and Hattie was almost one! I remember asking the maintenance staff from the Smith Center to put up a basketball goal over the garage. It was a glass backboard! The irony!

That fall, Jawad and Jackie visited campus. We always tried to bring recruits in for a home football game where we tailgated as a team and they could see the energy on campus. Jackie had already committed, so his job was to help recruit Jawad. Good players need good teammates if they want to win. Just as the football game started, I walked with Jawad and Jackie the long way around the outskirts of the field in the front of the fans. When we got in front of the student section, we walked through the crowd and the chants and screams began. UNC fans know. They know basketball. They know recruiting. They knew Jawad and Jackie and they cheered them on. Now Jawad and Jackie knew about the enthusiasm for Carolina basketball and it made them feel special. Jawad ended up committing to us soon thereafter.

One of my goals was to recruit the best players in North Carolina and make sure no one slipped through the cracks. I remember going to see Southern HS work out in Durham. There was a kid named David Noel who had committed to play football at UNC, and I wanted to see if he could help us on the basketball court. He was an impressive athlete with elite speed and quickness. He ended up coming over to Chapel Hill for an unofficial visit, and we talked in my office. David opened up and said he really wanted to focus on basketball! Unfortunately, we didn't have a scholarship available, but we discussed the option of "walking on" his first year and going on scholarship the rest of his career. I felt badly for the football staff, but basketball was in David's heart, and he ended up joining our team as a freshman "walk-on." He turned out to be quite a player for UNC and ended up playing in the NBA! Not a bad "walk on!"

One of the keys to attracting good players is having good players who were good guys. Our players were good young men. One of our best "recruiters" was Jason Capel. Jason was a good guy who immediately connected with our recruits. He and the other players made our jobs a lot easier.

Back in July, Doug Wojcik was excited about two prospects in particular—Rashad McCants and Sean May. I went to Los Angeles to evaluate an event. There was a big kid I wanted to see. As Roy taught me, you had to take in as much as you could with the limited time. I locked in on the big man, but positioned my chair between two courts so I could evaluate the second court when there was a stoppage in play. On Court 2, I saw this guard flying all over the court with tremendous energy and athleticism. After the first half, I decided to make Court 2 my primary game to evaluate. During a dead ball, I went to the scorer's table to find out where that team was from and who that athletic guard was. That team was from South Carolina and that guard was Raymond Felton. After the game, I asked the coach to call me and put Raymond on the phone. I offered him a scholarship. The rest is history!

With Jawad and Jackie committed in the fall, we ended up securing the commitments from Raymond, Sean, David and Rashad the next year. That group ended up leading UNC to the 2005 National Championship. Not a bad summer's work by my staff and me!

CHAPTER NINE:

MANAGING CHANGE

"When managing change, leaders must know
that people feel awkward when they try new things.
They are concerned more with what they are giving
up than what they are gaining and that they
personalize the change and feel alone."
—MARK COLE

Managing change is one of the trickiest things in business.

Dean Smith was one of the most successful coaches in the history of any team sport. Red Auerbach, John Wooden, Tom Landry, and Don Shula ... Dean Smith is in that class. At the time of his retirement in 1997 after thirty-six years as the head coach at UNC, Coach Smith had won an NCAA record of 879 games, won two NCAA Championships, coached in eleven Final Fours, won thirteen ACC Championships, won seventeen Regular Season ACC Championships, won one NIT Championship, led the USA to the 1976 Olympic Gold Medal, and 96 percent of his players received their degrees! Coach Smith was not only a great coach, he was truly a father figure to many of his players, regardless of race, age, or basketball ability.

Upon Coach Smith's retirement in October 1997, long-time assistant coach Bill Guthridge became the head coach at UNC. "Coach Gut," as he was popularly referred to by former players, joined Dean Smith in 1967 and was an assistant at UNC for thirty seasons!! He had many opportunities to leave to become a head coach at major universities, but he was more than happy to be Coach Smith's right-hand man for one of the nation's elite basketball programs.

The two men from Kansas attended rival universities, played for legendary coaches, and came together to lead UNC to unprecedented heights. Coach Smith was a 1953 graduate of the University of Kansas and Coach Gut was a 1960 graduate of Kansas State University. Interestingly, they both majored in mathematics. As a former player, that makes total sense. Coaches Smith and Guthridge both had sharp minds and analyzed everything like engineers—Coach Smith dissected opponents' defenses with precision, while Coach Gut would dissect how to operate the program with precision. Coach Smith would initiate the use of points per possession to gauge our offensive and defensive efficiency, while Coach Gut would initiate the use of off-season conditioning to improve our in-season performances.

Coach Smith and Coach Gut may have been the best head coach/assistant coach tandem in the history of sports! There was tremendous respect between them. True gentlemen who complemented each other seamlessly. Coach Smith ran the team. Coach Guthridge ran the program. Coach Smith didn't care much for spending time at the Carolina Basketball School. Coach Gut was there every hour of every day ... I could go on and on and on and on.

The consistency of Coach Smith and Coach Gut was reflected in their support staff. Eddie Fogler played at UNC for Coach Smith and Coach Gut, graduating in 1970 with a degree in ... yes ... mathematics! A year later, he became an assistant at UNC and stayed for fifteen years. Coach Fogler had one of the best minds I have ever been around. "Savvy" was one of Coach Smith's favorite terms, and Coach Fogler was full of savvy. His smarts were evident when Coach Smith would allow the assistants to add a comment during time-outs or at halftime. He was a good player from NYC and had a great career as a head coach.

Roy Williams was on the UNC staff when I played, too. He was an assistant there for ten years. Coach Williams was a man I got close to as a player. Oftentimes, the youngest assistant would get closest to the players because of their age, their ability to relate to the players, and their responsibilities would bring them around the team often, like overseeing the running program and checking class attendance.

Can you imagine ... Dean Smith, Bill Guthridge, Eddie Fogler, and Roy Williams ... all on one staff at the same time? How blessed were the players during that period!

In addition to the coaches, Marc Davis was the long-time trainer and still going strong since he was taping my ankles in the early 1980s. Linda Woods and Kay Thomas were two of the secretaries who were on staff when I played and were still there in 2000. Veterans Angela Lee and Ruth Kirkendall rounded out the administrative team, along with Armin Dastur. I had five secretaries in our office. Most basketball programs were lucky to have one! Carolina basketball was a huge operation.

Coach Smith and his staff did a magnificent job of creating "The Carolina Family." Every former player, coach, and manager were made to feel special by everyone. Every year, former players would get the basketball media guide with a handwritten note from Coach Smith. If you came to town for a game, Coach would always have a ticket for you. Linda Woods was his executive assistant, and she was a great gatekeeper. She had the most wonderful southern accent and was always very sweet and accommodating. Sometimes, you would call for Coach Smith and talk to Linda for several minutes, and when you hung up, you realized you may have not gotten what you really wanted, but she made you feel good about it! That was a talent.

"The Carolina Family" was real. It is real to this day. Some of my closest relationships in basketball are UNC players I DIDN'T play with. Recently, I played golf with John Kuester in Cary, NC. John was in the class of 1977, but when I came to Carolina in 1979, John was playing in the NBA. All the Carolina guys in the NBA would spend the summers in Chapel Hill to work on their games and hang out. It was an awesome experience for the current players to play with and against the NBA guys. John took me under his wing. We would go to old Woollen Gym and work on my shooting. John had a great shot and was a good teacher. We would play a lot of one-on-one. When John was the head coach at Boston University, I even drove from Long Island to get a workout with him.

Mitch Kupchak, Mike O'Koren, Woody Coley, Richard Vinroot, David Chadwick, Scott Williams, Shammond Williams, Makhtar N'Diaye, and Wes Miller ... these are all men who played at UNC in a different era from me who I consider friends. I recently connected with Scott Williams via Twitter. We exchanged tweets and I noticed his Twitter picture was of Joe Biden. I was doing a local radio show on WBT in Charlotte that discussed current events. Biden and Donald

Trump were the two Presidential candidates. The country was becoming very divided during the COVID-19 pandemic as there were several killings of black men at the hands of white police officers. Protests consumed America. The level of hate was strong. Biden vs. Trump. Left vs. Right. It was intense. I am very conservative and side with the Republican Party, but I wanted to learn from a supporter from the left, especially a black man. I wanted to try to learn from him and his experiences. I wanted to try to see things through his eyes. I sent Scott a direct message on Twitter asking for his telephone number. He quickly responded and later that day, we talked. I asked him about racism and his views on Trump. As our conversation was coming to a close, I told him Coach Smith must be looking down on us with pride as two former players of his from different eras and different races were talking politics together. In closing, I joked with Scott, saying, "We were on the phone for thirty-seven minutes. I asked you one question and you talked for thirty-six minutes!"

That's "The Carolina Family!"

Taking over a program that did not have significant change in its leadership for forty years while accumulating massive success can be overwhelming. It was a huge undertaking, even for a person who played there. I became the caretaker and leader of not just the current players and staff, but of an institution that had over 150 former players and millions of fans all loyal to UNC basketball. They were especially loyal to its architect, Dean Smith, and that man was still very much alive and resided in the same building that I worked in each and every day. A building bearing his name ... the Dean E. Smith Center!

One afternoon, Coach Smith and Coach Guthridge took me to lunch at the prestigious Carolina Club on campus. We all wore coats and ties. Coach Smith led Coach Guthridge and I into the dining area to be seated. I remember the pride I felt as we walked to our table. Here I am as the head coach of UNC getting ready to dine with the two legends who filled that role before me! We were the only living head coaches to lead Carolina basketball! As we sat down, Coach Smith, who sat across from me, said, "You know you were the fifth choice, don't you?" I was shocked and hurt. Why would he say such a thing? It was hard to enjoy the meal after that.

In September, our staff was as settled in their roles as we could be, given the circumstances. There was so much work to do and so many people to meet. Prioritizing the workload was challenging—recruiting, preparing for the start of the season, scheduling, meeting with alumni groups ... the list went on. One issue that needed immediate attention as we approached the season was tickets. Tickets to UNC games were coveted greatly. The arena accommodated 21,750 people, and as the head coach, I had access to three hundred of them. At Notre Dame, I only had access to about seventy-five tickets. I needed to meet with Coach Smith, Coach Guthridge, and Linda Woods to sort out the ticket and parking lists. Along with the tickets, there were about one hundred parking passes that had been assigned to the basketball program to use for recruiting, the players' guests, our families, and friends of the program. The list of friends of the program was extensive. There were people who had assigned seats and parking passes for many years. I was not looking forward to this day!

We sat in my office, the office that Dean Smith and Bill Guthridge had used as their own since the Smith Center had opened in 1986. Linda had the list of names with their number of seats, the seats location, and the location of the parking pass that each person had. Linda proceeded to go down the list and call out a name, the number of tickets they were assigned, the location and the respective parking pass. We would look at each other and decide if that person kept their seats and parking pass or if we would move them to another location, reduce the number of tickets, change their parking spot, or eliminate them from the list. It was a stressful exercise, as there were people on those lists for thirty years! Tickets and parking passes were like gold in North Carolina. Many people had their status tied to those tickets and parking passes. We finally got through that difficult process, but I could tell it wasn't easy on anyone.

As the month of September continued, I could tell some of my administrative staff weren't happy with me and my staff. With all the changes, it was unsettling. Linda and Ruth told me they were retiring. The timing was unfortunate, as the season was upon us. After they decided to leave, they ended up working for Coach Smith and Coach Guthridge in their office in the bottom of the Smith Center. This was unsettling for me. Having Coach Smith and Coach Guthridge in the building was a blessing and a curse. They were great resources for me. I would talk basketball with Coach Smith, and he would meet with recruits. Coach Guthridge knew how the program ran better than anyone. However, some disgruntled people—administrative staff, former players, and season ticket holders— now had a place to voice their displeasure.

Now I had to add hiring an executive secretary to my list of things to do. I ended up hitting a home run with the addition of Jennifer Holbrook. Her husband was the assistant baseball coach. Jennifer was a welcome addition to our team, but she was in for a challenging road taking over during that hectic time while replacing a significant figure in the program. Her poise, grace, and competitiveness showed through. We were lucky to find her. She ended up working for Roy for many years before her husband took the head coaching position at the University of South Carolina. I am grateful for her work and friendship.

There were a lot of rumors that I was changing the culture of the UNC basketball program, and not for the better. Rumors of former players being unhappy because I didn't retain the former assistant coaches. Talk that I disrespected friends of the program by moving their seats and parking passes. Rumors that I was putting up pictures of myself in the office. That was the picture of Michael hitting "The Shot." Rumors I was taking down pictures of the former ACC Championship teams. We were renovating the locker room and the workers temporarily removed the pictures so they wouldn't be damaged during the renovation.

There was a lot of negative noise, and we haven't even started playing the games!

CHAPTER TEN:

THE FIRST SEASON

"A wise man adapts himself to circumstances,
as water shapes itself to the vessel that contains it."
—CHINESE PROVERB

UNC had a reputation of being a "soft" program, and I wanted to instill a toughness like we did at Notre Dame. We had good talent in my first year, but I felt we needed to become a grittier team. As I witnessed in studying video from the previous season, there was a lack of toughness vs. Duke and Michigan State. Michigan State had manhandled the Tar Heels in Chapel Hill. The culture had been somewhat casual, as players weren't required to lift weights and it was easy for them to get out of practice. The problem was they had success. The prior year, although they struggled some during the regular season, they made it to the Final Four! They had talent.

We had tough pre-season workouts, as I believed you can control certain things as a coach. One of the things you can control was being in top physical condition. In one of our early running sessions, a player started to struggle and motioned to Marc Davis. He ran over to the player to assist him. I yelled at Marc to back off and challenged the player to finish the sprints. I didn't want players quitting when things got tough. There is a difference between being hurt and being injured. This player was hurting. To his credit, he stayed on the court and finished the workout. My job as a coach was to push players out of their comfort zones to put them and the team in position to accomplish great things. Just like we did at Notre Dame.

About a month later was the official start of practice. Our first practice went well. There was great energy and the team was emotionally invested. Players were diving on the floor and I would run over with their teammates to help pick them up. Coaching my alma mater on the Smith Center floor where Dean Smith and Bill Guthridge led so many great teams gave me a feeling of great pride. At the conclusion of practice, we huddled up and everyone put their hands together and I said, "One, two, three … Irish!" Oops!

We struggled some in our early games. Even though we had a team coming off the Final Four, we missed the talented point guard play of Ed Cota. Ed was a tremendous talent who was one of the best passers I ever saw. Freshman Adam Boone filled the vacant point guard position and started alongside Joe Forte, Jason Capel, Kris Lang, and Brendan Haywood. We lost at Michigan State and at home to Kentucky. Those games weren't very close. These are the types of games the UNC faithful was used to winning!

After exams, Ronald Curry and Julius Peppers joined the team, coming over from the football team. Fortunately for us, the football team didn't make it to a bowl game, so they were able to join the basketball team around Christmas. Immediately, I could see their talent. Extremely strong and athletic. They were two of our better players! Julius was a key player in helping UNC make the Final Four run the prior year, and Ronald was a high school All-American in basketball.

Ronald was quickly inserted into the starting lineup and gave us the point guard play necessary to compete against the best teams in the country. Julius gave us a talented player off the bench to back up Kris and Brendan. They added a toughness, savvy, and athleticism that we needed. As a result, we beat UCLA in Pauley Pavilion and continued on an eighteen-game winning streak, one of the longest winning streaks in Carolina history!

Obviously, the big game on the schedule was Duke. UNC hadn't won at Duke in five years. My parents came to visit for the month of February and my brother, John, came down for the game. John and my dad sat right behind me in the front row behind the bench in Cameron Indoor Stadium. After halftime, I came out onto the court and saw my dad sitting on the front row with his head in his hands, looking tired. Concerned, I asked John, "Is Dad all right?" John responded, "Is Dad all right? He just copped the best seat in the house!" My dad sat next to my assistants on the bench for the entire second half, looking like one of the coaches!

Like most UNC-Duke games, it was tight throughout. In the final minutes of the game, there was a time-out and we were leading, but Duke was making a push. As Coach Smith always did, I wanted to keep my team loose. I said to them, "You know … one thing hasn't changed … Duke still has the ugliest cheerleaders in the ACC!" They laughed. They were loose and confident. We ended up winning on Brendan Haywood's two free throws with one second on the clock!

At that time I was a young immature coach trying to connect with my players. But I look back on that comment about the Duke cheerleaders and cringe. As a leader of young men and a father to a young daughter I should have found another comment to keep my team loose. Coach Smith would never had said that, but he always found a way to keep us loose in tight games.

I told the team before the game, "When we beat Duke, we won't celebrate on the court. Act like you expected to win!" To their credit, they didn't celebrate. We walked over and shook hands and proceeded calmly into the tiny visitor's locker room. When we all gathered, we danced around like little kids!

I have a picture in my office of the bench with my dad sitting there next to the assistant coaches. Brendan had just hit the game-winning free throws. The coaches were stoic. My dad had a smile on his face. My brother had his fists in the air as he celebrated with the small contingent of UNC supporters. What a memory!

We beat Duke at Duke, and when the rankings came out, we were ranked number one in the country!

The next evening, I was home watching CNN-SI on TV late into the night. It was a new sports show competing with ESPN. They had three people debating the appropriateness of my comment about the Duke cheerleaders! How did they know? Apparently, one of my players told his brother and word got out. I wrote a letter to Coach K and the Duke cheerleading coach apologizing for my remarks. A few days later, I received a message that the cheerleading coach called. As I was driving on Franklin Street, I was returning calls and contacted her. I held my breath as the phone was ringing, anticipating I was going to get chewed out. When she finally answered, she said, "Matt, this is Theresa. You may not remember me, but we were in class together at Carolina." I immediately remembered her. Theresa was in several of my classes and she was a cheerleader for our teams in the early 1980s. We exchanged pleasantries, and she forgave me for my comments.

As we were on our winning streak, I felt we weren't getting better. I could see it on film, but it is hard to convince a team that they need to continue to focus and work hard to improve during such a winning streak. I remember beating Wake Forest on the road in a close game. We played poorly, and I got on the team afterward. I told them, "We won because we are more talented … not because we played better!" They weren't happy, but I knew we needed to focus on getting better each day.

Next up was a talented Maryland team that we had already beaten on the road. There was a front-page article that came out the day before the game about junior Jason Capel. It stated that he was a great "role player" for our team. I met with Jason before our practice in the coaches' locker room and discussed the article. I was happy for him, but I could tell that he wasn't! I was puzzled, but quickly realized that he didn't like being referred to as a "role player." Jason was highly recruited and being considered a "role player" was viewed as disrespectful, that he wasn't of star quality. During the game the next day, I felt Jason was forcing things to prove that he was more than a "role player." There was a time-out and I "got on him" about forcing things in front of the team. Then I said something along the lines of, "And you didn't like being referred to as a 'role player'…" As those words came out of my mouth and I saw his head drop, I knew right away I made a mistake. I broke a trust with him that I don't think I ever got back! That is a "coaching scar" I live with to this day.

We went on to beat Maryland and Jason ended up scoring a career-high twenty-seven points, but we still weren't getting better.

Next up was a game at Clemson. They played a triangle and two defense and we never got in a rhythm. We were down ten points with ten seconds left in the game and their coach, Larry Shyatt, called a time-out! Their crowd was going crazy and Larry ran into the stands to hug his wife! I was fuming in the huddle, as I felt totally disrespected. You don't call a time-out that late in a game with the lead in hand. I told our team we would have a chance to pay them back ... and we did!

Just a few weeks later, we faced Clemson in the first round of the ACC Tournament in Atlanta. We were motivated to "pay them back" for the embarrassment at Clemson. We had a sizable lead in the second half. With seconds to go, I joked with my staff, "Should I call time-out?" I didn't. When the horn sounded, I went over to shake hands with Larry Shyatt and said, "I asked my assistants if I should call time-out with ten seconds to go and they said, 'No'". Larry went ballistic!

Larry and I have since joked about that moment.

You gotta love the ACC!

We ended up playing Duke in the ACC finals. Before the game, Dick Vitale visited with me on the court. He really pushed for me to stay at Notre Dame. He was a big ND fan, and we had gotten into a heated exchange on the phone the day I left Notre Dame for Chapel Hill. I told him at center court that "this" is one of the reasons I took the job! Implying that you get to play on the biggest stage in college basketball!

Unfortunately, we got blown out by Duke. It wasn't pretty. As I stated earlier, we weren't getting better and it showed in that game. The momentum of the season flipped on us and it was hard to get it back.

That week, we were given a number two seed in the NCAA Tournament and faced a dangerous Princeton team in New Orleans. Princeton was a team no one wanted to play because of their unique style and their history of upsets under Pete Carril. John Thompson III was their coach now, and he did a great job. After we ate our pre-game meal, we went over our scouting report. When the report was done, I wanted to make sure we were emotionally ready, so I punched the whiteboard for emphasis! We played well and won, but my hand was killing me!

Two days later, we faced Penn State. Ironically, the year before, my Notre Dame team beat Penn State in the NIT semifinals easily. They had everyone back, but we were North Carolina and were a top-ranked team. We were expected to win. However, Penn State was an experienced team, and they played loose and with a lot of confidence. We seemed sluggish and could never find a rhythm. It was a heartbreaking loss that ended our season.

CHAPTER ELEVEN:

THERE IS NO OFFSEASON

"Every day you come to work,
five things will happen you didn't anticipate."
—BILL PARCELLS

I was playing golf with Coach Smith and Coach Guthridge at Governors Club in Chapel Hill. We had finished a season that had some great moments—an eighteen-game winning streak, beating Duke at Duke, winning the ACC Regular Season Title, being named AP National Coach of the Year, and recruiting had gone well. I was trying to enjoy some time away from the stress of the season and recruiting. It had been a taxing year. I really enjoyed being with those men. It was an honor to spend time with them. When the round was over, I pulled my cell phone out of my golf bag and, as usual, there were a lot of voice mails! I listened to a message about Joe Forte possibly going pro! Joe was a sophomore All-American. He had a terrific year and was our best returning player. So much for a relaxing spring!

I attended the Final Four that year. It was crazy. As the head coach, I got to stay in the main hotel, and as the head coach at UNC, everyone wants a piece of you. You can't walk through the hotel lobby without getting stopped multiple times. It was all-consuming just to get from the elevator to the front door. Fans wanting your autograph and aspiring young coaches wanting a job. Then one person came up to me and said, "You know Joe is going pro!"

What!

It turns out that Joe had decided to go pro. It's funny how the head coach is sometimes the last to know. I thought he should come back and play point guard for us in preparation for his future. Point guard was probably the position he would need to learn how to play for his best chance of having a good NBA career. However, he and his mother decided to enter the draft.

On top of all of that, rumors continued to circulate about the pictures in the basketball facility and of disgruntled former players

This was unsettling, to say the least.

CHAPTER TWELVE:

DEALING WITH FAILURE

"There are no great victories in life
without overcoming great adversity."
—WOODY HAYES

As I told Dick Baddour during the interview process, "My first year we are going to be good, my second we are going to be bad, and the third year we will rebuild."

We really struggled my second year. Brendan Haywood and Joe Forte were playing in the NBA and Ronald Curry and Julius Peppers decided to focus on preparing for the NFL Draft. We started Adam Boone, Jackie Manuel, Jawad Williams, Kris Lang, and Jason Capel. We had three inexperienced players, and we weren't very big or athletic. That is not a good recipe for success. After every loss, I had to stand in front of a bank of microphones in front of a packed room of reporters and answer questions about another loss. I was never going to throw our players "under the bus," nor was I going to blame the previous staff for the team I inherited. Dean Smith would never cast blame on anyone but himself after a loss. I continued to say that we needed to focus on getting better. As legendary football coach Paul Brown once said, "When you win, say nothing. When you lose, say less."

We lost to Davidson at home. They were still coached by Bob McKillop. Having worked for him at Davidson, along with our long-standing friendship, it was a difficult game for both of us. He knew the impact that loss would have on me. UNC isn't supposed to lose, especially at home, especially to a team from a mid-major conference like the Southern Conference.

We got blown out at Maryland. It wasn't close. UNC was a game everyone circled on their calendars, and with us struggling, there would be no mercy. I just had to take the punches and come off the mat each and every day. It is very important for a leader to show strength and hope during crisis. That is what I tried to show, even though my insides were hurting.

We played Duke at home and they had us by twenty plus points most of the second half, but Coach K held the ball and had his team back off. After the game, I shook his hand and thanked him for not running up the score. He said, "I have been there." Classy gesture from a legendary rival! Coach K struggled in his first three years at Duke. I played against those teams. He knew better than anyone what I was going through.

We had to face Duke again in the first round of the ACC Tournament in Charlotte. I knew we had to do something drastic to have a chance to win. We had a week to prepare, and I told my staff we were going to hold the ball until the last ten seconds of the shot clock, then we would run one of five new plays we would put in that week. I was taking a page out of Coach Smith's playbook.

First, I needed buy-in from our leader. I met with senior Jason Capel and told him my thoughts on how I believed we needed to play to have a chance to beat Duke. I needed his support to "sell it" to his teammates. Jason was a smart player whose dad was a successful college coach. He understood and supported the decision.

My staff and I worked on the plays in the Smith Center before we worked with the team. We practiced this new strategy all week. We were ready. The team came out against Duke and executed the plan very well. You could sense the crowd's uneasiness in the Charlotte Coliseum as we held the ball, passing up open opportunities until we went into our sets late in the shot clock. The game was close at halftime. In the second half, we got down about ten points and the crowd grew restless, but I told the team to stay the course. We got back in the game and cut their lead to five points late in the contest. Then there was a critical call by an official that went against us with about five minutes to go that broke our backs and we lost. I was proud of our team in defeat.

Our season was over. We finished 8-20. It was the worst record in Carolina basketball history. My name was on it, but I was tough enough to deal with it. Plus, I knew help was on the way!

CHAPTER THIRTEEN:

THREE FRESHMEN AND TWO SOPHOMORES

"Good habits formed at youth make all the difference."
—ARISTOTLE

We welcomed a great recruiting class led by Raymond Felton, Sean May, and Rashad McCants. Several players transferred that summer, as they saw the writing on the wall that they would probably not play significant roles on the team. However, that only fed into the narrative that people weren't happy with how I was running the program, and the rumors persisted.

As we approached the start of non-conference play, I debated on starting three freshmen. Rashad wasn't a great practice player, but he was talented. Will Johnson was a senior and a great leader. I considered starting him, but I felt that starting three freshmen along with two sophomores in Jawad Williams and Jackie Manuel was the way to go. Not many teams started such a young group then, but I felt they were the future of our program and I needed to let them grow together.

We opened up with the Pre-season NIT and played Rutgers at home. Rashad was terrific. When "the lights were on," he flourished. We were down late in the game, but had a great comeback win that energized the Smith Center.

We ended up making it to New York City to play in Madison Square Garden. Growing up on Long Island made it extra special for me. My whole family was there, along with many friends. However, we had to face Roy Williams and the Kansas Jayhawks in the semifinals. Kansas was loaded with talent. They had just come off a Final Four appearance, and this Kansas team ended up going back to the Final Four that year.

Having worked for Roy Williams for seven years at Kansas, I knew how he coached as well as anyone. I told our team how we were going to play and worked on it in practice in NYC. We were going to spread the floor, move the ball, and drive it to the basket. No set plays. We needed to control the tempo against the fast-paced Jayhawks. I felt some pushback during practice. The body language on a couple of key players told me that they weren't pleased with this adjustment. I sat them down at the end of the gym. I pulled up a chair, as I wanted to get down to their level and not verbally or physically talk down to them. I spoke "with them." I could tell we connected. Assistant Doug Wojcik told me later that was "good coaching." I appreciated that and was proud of the way it was handled.

The next day in a packed Madison Square Garden, the players executed beautifully as we went into the half with a nice lead. We had Kansas on the ropes.

As I walked onto the court for the second half, my mother came up from her seat behind the bench and said,

"Congratulations!" I said, "Mom, we have another half to go!" Gotta love Mary Doherty!

We stuck with our game plan in the second half, as we didn't run one set play. We put the players in position to play basketball and won going away! It was a proud moment for me winning against my mentor Roy Williams and Kansas in Madison Square Garden with Dick Vitale announcing the game on ESPN!

We couldn't celebrate too long because two nights later, we had to face Stanford in the championship game! The players were starting to believe in the staff and themselves. We executed our defensive game plan very well in taking Stanford out of their sets that they ran so well. After winning that game, we went from being unranked to number twelve in the national polls starting three freshmen and two sophomores!

Carolina basketball is back!

Meg, Nan, Maureen, and me. John was a late arrival.

John eventually showed up in East Meadow, NY.

*St. Raphael's Little League Baseball. I am in the back
row, the last player on the right.*

*With Paul Eibeler and my brother John.
I am on the left.*

"Gates to Heaven." Prospect Park.

Why I love basketball.

*1976 St. Raphael's CYO Nassau Co Champs. #24 back
row. #20 front row was MLB player Gene Larkin.*

*1976-77 Holy Trinity team. I am in back row far left.
Coach Bob McKillop on far right.*

1980 McDonald's All American picture with John Wooden.

1980 State Champs. Dick Zeitler in back row on left.
Brother John in front row on right.

1982 Pre-Practice huddle.

*1982 National Championship post game
interview with the starting five.*

Proof I could actually dunk!

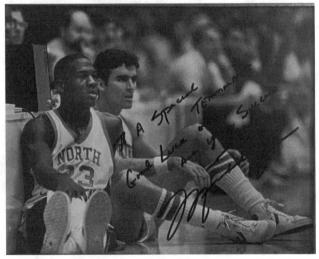

Michael and me waiting to check into a game in Chapel Hill. He autographed the picture for me.

Michael and me, Spring 1984.

*Roommate and lifelong friend Bobby
Ellington and me at graduation, 1984.*

Sam Perkins and me at graduation.

Honored to be a part of the great Carolina Basketball tradition.

Sports Illustrated, *November 30, 1981.*

"The Shot" by Michael Jordan. Yours truly at the foul line.

THE84DRAFT

1 H. OLAJUWON	8 L. GORDON	15 T. STANSBURY	22 T. SEWELL	51 J. PETERSEN
2 S. BOWIE	9 O. THORPE	16 J. STOCKTON	23 E. JONES	70 R. CARLISLE
3 M. JORDAN	10 L. WOOD	17 J. TURNER	24 M. YOUNG	131 O. SCHMIDT
4 S. PERKINS	11 K. WILLIS	18 V. FLEMING	27 R. ANDERSON	156 K. BANNISTER
5 C. BARKLEY	12 T. McCORMICK	19 B. THOMPSON	33 S. COLTER	84 OTHERS
6 M. TURPIN	13 J. HUMPHRIES	20 T. CAMPBELL	39 D. YOUNG	
7 A. ROBERTSON	14 M. CAGE	21 K. FIELDS	46 J. KERSEY	

Tough Day. The 1984 Draft.

1999 Notre Dame media guide.

Working with Tucker at UNC holiday clinic.

*Bench and fan reaction as Brendan Haywood hit winning
free throws at Duke 2001. Brother John is behind the
bench with NC t-shirt with fists raised and Dad is sitting
on bench next to assistant David Cason. Memories!*

*Post game handshake with Coach K after UNC
win in Chapel Hill.*

Holding Tucker upon return to South Bend after a big road win.

Confronting Duke assistant Chris Collins in Chapel Hill.
Rashad McCants looks on.

Coach Williams and me before the UNC/Kansas
game in Madison Square Garden Nov, 2002.
I worked for Roy for seven years at Kansas.

*Golf with President Bush, John Heidtke,
and Mickey Holden in Dallas.*

*David Noel, Sean May, me, Jackie Manuel, Melvin Scott,
and Raymond Felton in the front at UNC reunion.*

UNC head coaches pictured in the locker room.

*Tucker wearing his dad's old jersey number
in a playoff victory at Charlotte Catholic.*

*Tucker attacking the rim and his "old man" in his
back yard at college in Louisville, KY.*

Big Game James Worthy with Hattie and Kelly at a reunion.

*Kelly and me on the "Carolina Blue Carpet"
at UNC Basketball reunion.*

*Matt McKillop, me, Bob McKillop, and Bob's father-in-law,
Mr. Cunningham at NYC event honoring Bob.
Great coach. Great friend. Great man.*

*NYC Knick great Walt Frazier and me before
Hornet game in Charlotte.*

Notre Dame star and great friend Ryan Humphrey.

The Carolina Family at the 2017 Final Four.

Getting ready for UNC Watch Party with Zoey and Zorro.

Challenge Coin given to me by Lt. Colonel Matt Karres.

Clinic at St. Raphael's 2019.

Corporate keynote talk 2020.

Great friend John Black with Kelly and me at Grandfather Mountain, NC.

Nobody had better parents.

Family trip to Niagara Falls.

Family vacation.

Hattie signs rowing scholarship to UNC.

Hattie is a Tar Heel!

CHAPTER FOURTEEN:

THE BREAK

"Setbacks are an opportunity for growth."
—MATT DOHERTY

We were back in Madison Square Garden for the Holiday Festival during the Christmas holiday and faced Iona in the first game. They were a scrappy team led by Head Coach Jeff Ruland. Jeff was a star player on Long Island when I was growing up, and he played at Iona for Jim Valvano. We had already won our first ACC game at Florida State before we broke for Christmas, so we were in a good mental state.

The game had started, and we were trying to get the rust out from the short layoff. Then all of a sudden, starting center Sean May went down with a foot injury. He was helped off the court. I checked with trainer Marc Davis at halftime. Sean was done for the game. We ended up losing to Iona. To make matters worse, we learned after the game that Sean fractured a bone in his foot. He was going to be out of the lineup for several weeks. This was a big blow, as we didn't have much depth at his position.

We were able to rebound two nights later and beat St. John's in the third place game of the Holiday Festival, but there was a definite concern about how we were going to cope going forward without Sean in the lineup as ACC play resumed.

I ended up starting 6-5 sophomore David Noel in Sean's place. We were forced to play with three guards and two forwards, but that is coaching. Leaders need to figure out a way to try to turn a negative into a positive. We needed to play more aggressively on defense and push the ball on offense, relying on our speed and quickness.

We struggled in ACC play without Sean. We got blown out at Maryland in the worst loss in Carolina history. No one was going to feel sorry for Carolina. Teams were going to pour it on us if they could and the Terps did just that. Coach K had some compassion for me. Maryland Coach Gary Williams, not so much! It was tough being on the sidelines getting beaten like we were. I remember putting my hand in my pocket and fiddling with a challenge coin my good friend Matt Karres had given me. Matt is a dear friend I met in Chapel Hill. He was a lieutenant colonel in the US Army. He gave me that coin and I would carry it as a reminder of my appreciation of the men and women who sacrificed for our great country. As I fiddled with the coin, I said to myself, "It could be worse. I could be in Afghanistan."

Perspective is important during difficult times!

We played a talented UConn team at home and won in an exciting game. The Smith Center was rocking. We got off to a great start. I had coached several times vs. Jim Calhoun's teams. First as an assistant at KU and then as the head coach at Notre Dame. We had a lot of success against their press, and they often struggled against our zone defenses. We were up big in the first half, but UConn roared back and took the lead with about 1:30 to go in the game. I called time-out. We drew up a set play for Raymond to use a fake ball screen. Jawad set a pick for Rashad along the baseline, sending him into the post. If Rashad wasn't open, Raymond would look to Jawad coming off a down pick. Raymond read it correctly and hit Jawad for what was the game-winning basket! It was a huge win for us against a great opponent.

We even beat Duke at home! We were still without Sean, so we went with a similar game plan to the one we used against Kansas in NYC. We were going "five out" to spread the floor and attack the basket against Duke's pressure defense. Turn their strength into their weakness. As usual against rival Duke, it was a tight game. This were close throughout. The intensity in the Smith Center was typical of a Carolina–Duke contest. With about five minutes to go in the game, Raymond knocked the ball out of Dahntay Jones' hand as he went up for a shot. Dahntay violently flailed his arms and hit Raymond right in the face. Raymond went down to the floor. Raymond is one of the toughest players I ever coached, so when he stayed on the floor, I knew he was hurt. As I went over to check on Raymond in front of the Duke bench, I complained to the officials about Jones hitting Raymond in the face. Duke assistant Chris Collins came off the bench and yelled to the officials, "Is he checking on his player or complaining about the call?" I didn't think an assistant coach should do such a thing. I charged at Collins. We went toe-to-toe, yelling at each other. As we were in each other's chests, I was thinking, "With twenty-two thousand people in the stands and millions watching on TV, what do we do now?" With that, one of their players came off the bench and pushed me in the chest! Realizing this was getting out of control, I backed up with my hands in the air to show that we all needed to calm down. My players came over and pushing ensued. Raymond was in the middle of it with blood pouring down his face.

Cooler heads prevailed and we went back to our benches. The tone was set for an exciting finish. Raymond went to the locker room to get stitched up and he game back into the game with tremendous determination, leading us to a dramatic win. You gotta love Raymond!

We ended up facing Maryland in the first round of the ACC Tournament in Greensboro. Maryland had dominated us in the last matchup in College Park, MD. We came out with great poise and played terrific basketball taking it to the Terps, resulting in a great win! It was one the biggest turnarounds in Carolina history, losing by fifty-three points at Maryland, then beating them by twelve in Greensboro.

We now had to face Duke again in the semifinals. There was a lot of talk about Sean May's readiness to come back to action in recent weeks. He had been practicing well, but hadn't been cleared to play at that point. I met with Sean the night before and he desperately wanted to play. I wanted him to play! But he needed to clear it with his father, Scott. Scott was a legendary player at Indiana, winning the 1976 NCAA Championship under Bob Knight.

Sean got the okay to play! Do I start him? Does he come off the bench? We just beat Duke without him.

These are the decisions that test a leader! There will always be tremendous scrutiny around key decisions like this.

Before the game, I came out for the early warmups and saw Duke assistant Johnny Dawkins. Johnny was a great player at Duke. We played against each other in high school and college. I liked Johnny and went over to shake his hand. As I extended my hand, he said with his arms folded, "That was f***ed up!" He was referring to my heated exchange with Chris Collins in the recent game in Chapel Hill. As I realized he was not going to shake my hand, I extended it farther and turned my body so the media across the court could see us. I smiled with my hand extended long enough for everyone to get a good look. Then I walked away, continuing to smile.

Johnny and I laugh at that exchange now. When I see him, I extend my hand, asking him if he is going to shake it, and we laugh. He is a good guy and a good coach.

You gotta love the ACC!

I ended up deciding to have Sean come off the bench. When he entered the game, there was great excitement throughout the arena. Sean got the ball in the post and quickly turned for his classic jump hook that went into the basket! However, you could tell that he didn't have his wind yet for a game of that pace.

We lost to Duke. Coach K made the appropriate adjustments from our previous game. That is one of the many reasons he is a Hall of Fame coach.

We went back to Chapel Hill knowing we would not make the NCAA Tournament for the second year in a row. We did get a deserved invitation to play in the NIT, however. Wyoming was our first-round opponent and we played at home. It was an exciting game, which we won. The crowd was very supportive even though we didn't make the NCAA Tournament. I really appreciated our fans, as all throughout the season, they were very supportive.

Our next opponent was Georgetown. We played them in the Smith Center. We were behind in the second half and ended up losing. A funny feeling came over me late in the contest that this may be my last game as the coach at North Carolina.

CHAPTER FIFTEEN:

THE END

"Coaching is nothing more than eliminating mistakes before you get fired."
—LOU HOLTZ

There were a lot of rumblings during the season of players not being happy. There was a rumor that Sean might transfer to Texas Tech to play for Bobby Knight. Dick Baddour came to my office in January to tell me that the media had requested our phone records (Open Records Act) and that "there were two calls to Lawrence, KS, and one to Lubbock, TX." He said in a nervous manner, "I had to talk with Roy about NCAA Championship Committees." I responded, "You are allowed to talk with Roy." He noted the call to Lubbock because of the rumor regarding Sean. I told him I would talk with Sean.

I called Sean into my office to discuss the call. He seemed disheartened that I was asking him if he called the Texas Tech offices. He said, "If I was going to call Coach Knight, I would use my cell phone." I could tell he was disappointed that I would ask him about it. My trust with him was damaged.

That was another moment I wish I had back. It was a definite "coaching scar." Sean was, and is, a great young man, and fortunately, we have a good relationship today.

As it turned out, Dean Smith had called Lubbock! He called to talk with a reporter who was doing a story on Bob Knight! How dumb was I!

After the Georgetown game, I asked Dick to meet with our team. I wanted him to help manage their emotions and control the narrative as we headed into the spring. I didn't want any fallout with the players that I experienced in previous years. I trusted that he would settle the team down if there were any issues.

I called him the next day and asked with confidence, "How did it go?" Dick replied, "Not so well." Not expecting that reaction, I responded, "What do you mean, 'Not so well?'" We decided to meet in the office to talk further. In that meeting, Dick couldn't look me in the eye. He was very uncomfortable. I asked him what happened in the meeting. I came to find out the dean of students attended the meeting. Dick mentioned some of the players weren't happy and were thinking of transferring. I mentioned that most players think of transferring right after the season, especially young players. His job was to settle them down.

I wondered why the dean of students had to be there? Dick brought up one incident of me calling a player a "pussy." I told him about the time in a practice when a player got hit in the groin and I couldn't see him for several minutes, as practice was going on. He was sitting behind the goal. Players get hit in the groin all the time. I went up to the player and said, "Don't be a pussy. Do you think Duke cares if you get hit in the groin?" Meaning that in a game, you may get hurt, but you have to get back into action as soon as possible. When the word "pussy" came out of my mouth, I realized right then that it was a poor choice of words. It was the only time I used that word all year and I regret using it to this day. "Coaching scar."

My conversation with Dick continued down a bad path. I felt this was the end. I said to Dick, "You know you are going to bring Roy in here, and if these players think I am tough, wait until he is the coach!"

I couldn't believe my career at UNC was crashing down so fast. It felt surreal. Our conversation quickly turned to my contract. I had three years left on my agreement and expected UNC to pay it in full. However, when I signed the contract, there was a clause in it that didn't guarantee all the money, only my base pay. I mentioned to Dick at the time I signed the contract that I didn't like that clause. He said it was put in because of the large buyout Jim Valvano received when he left NC State. Since we were part of the UNC school system, all the state schools had similar clauses. In addition, I told Dick when I was hired that I needed a seven-year contract, since Notre Dame offered me a ten-year contract. At the time, I was told that the state wouldn't agree to anything beyond six years, but he would give me a one-year extension after my first season. After my first season, I approached Dick about the extension and he told me he couldn't give it to me because the state board wasn't meeting that year.

I felt helpless. Where do I turn? How do I face my wife? How do I face my staff?

Finally, they organized a press conference announcing my "resignation." Dick asked me if I wanted to attend the conference. Dean Smith offered to join me as a sign of support. I had no desire to be present at that conference. I didn't want to resign, and I couldn't fake it.

I sat in my office as the head coach of North Carolina for the last time, dumbfounded. What went wrong? What was going on behind my back? What do I do now? Through all that chaos, who was there? Bobby Ellington! Bobby had talked to my wife and planned to meet me at the Smith Center to escort me through the swarm of media members who waited outside. My car was in the parking lot, so Bobby drove his car on the other side of the arena. I took a different route out of the arena and Bobby was waiting there in his running car. I skirted a few members of the media, jumped in his car, and he drove me home. That's a great friend!

I remember walking into my house. My wife was sitting on the edge of our bed with ESPN on the TV. I told her not to watch the press conference. I knew nothing good would come out of it. However, the press conference quickly started and now we were both sitting on the edge of the bed watching it. We were upset as my character and leadership came into question. I was shocked. How could the university I loved turn on me like this? How could Coach Smith allow this to happen? I left a great situation at Notre Dame to come "home" to help "The Family" in need and now I am being publicly shamed on national TV.

I felt like someone took a knife and cut my chest wide open for the whole world to see.

CHAPTER SIXTEEN:

FREE FALL

*"It is sometimes a mistake to climb; it is always
a mistake never even to make the attempt.
If you do not climb, you will not fall. This is true.
But is it that bad to fail, that hard to fall?"*
—NEIL GAIMAN

I remember Coach Smith calling me at home. He said, "If you only won twenty games. It is hard to fire a coach with twenty wins." I remember holding the phone away from my face, looking at it in dismay. We finished the year with nineteen wins, had great young talent and the most powerful man in the state of North Carolina was telling me that he couldn't save me over one win!

In every career decision I made, I always had Coach Smith and Roy Williams there for wise counsel. That was the Carolina Family. Now I felt like I was falling backward off the Empire State Building with no safety net to catch me.

CHAPTER SEVENTEEN:

AFTERMATH

*"You can't follow your heart when
it is more confused than your head."*
—Unknown

When you go through painful experiences, your true friends surface. People like Bobby Ellington, John Black, Steve Luquire, Michael Jordan, Kevin Huggins, Kevin White, and my family were all there to give me emotional support at the toughest time of my career.

Bobby was my college roommate. He was there the night I got hired and was there the day I "resigned." John Black and Steve Luquire dropped everything and came to my house to game plan on how to manage the narrative and plan for the future. Michael called and left me a long message expressing his disappointment and how I left a great job at Notre Dame to come back to Chapel Hill. Kevin Huggins stayed by my side and took Kelly and our family to the beach to get away with him and his wife, Vicki. Kevin White called me! Here was the director of athletics at Notre Dame, the school I left three years prior, calling me as a friend. I will never forget his wise words, "Take the high road. There is less traffic up there." I have tried to follow his advice every day since 2003.

Kelly was a rock during that time. She is a very loving mother and spouse. She is great in crisis, as she has good instincts. She had one concern and that was taking care of our family. We took Tucker and Hattie to the beach with the Huggins to get our minds right.

I remember calling my mother from Kevin Huggins' car on our way to Charlotte to do an interview with ESPN's Jay Bilas. When I finally got to hear her voice, I got emotional. She was obviously very disappointed in UNC, stating, "How could Coach Smith allow this to happen?" She wanted to write him a letter. I told her not to, but my mother did.

Fans see the fanfare of college athletics. They see the exciting games on ESPN. The bands. The cheerleaders. The crowds with painted faces. But they don't see the fallout from ugly separations. One such experience is the finality of the "resignation." As the head coach of major programs, you get many perks—nice cars, country club memberships, cell phones, support staff, and access to private jets. This was all about to go away!

Assistant Athletic Director Willy Scroggs was a great guy. He was a legendary lacrosse coach at UNC when I was a student. They won multiple championships, and I always enjoyed his good-natured disposition. Willy was in charge of the courtesy cars for the athletic department. My wife had a nice Lincoln Navigator and I drove a beautiful white BMW 750IL. Willy called me and said he needed to pick up my car and that he would give me a rental car for a period of time until I bought my own car. I lived in a great house on Chapel Hill Country Club at the end of a long cul-de-sac. The road extended right into my driveway. I imagine Willy was nervous for the awkward moment, but he didn't show it. He was the perfect person to execute this difficult task. After exchanging small talk, I took a cardboard box and gathered my personal items from the car—sunglasses, CDs, pads, pens, etc. As I held the box, I shook Willy's hand and proceeded to watch him pull out of my driveway in "my" beautiful BMW. I saw him for a few hundred yards down the long street. Finally, the brake lights came on and he turned right. "My car" and "my career" at UNC was officially over.

Weird. Just two seasons ago, I was voted 2001 AP National Coach of the Year and now I am out of a job!

What next?

CHAPTER EIGHTEEN:

MY LEADERSHIP JOURNEY

"You either get bitter or you get better.
It's that simple. You either take what has been
dealt to you and allow it to make you a better person,
or you allow it to tear you down. The choice does
not belong to fate, it belongs to you."
—JOSH SHIPP

John Black suggested I meet with Carol Weber at the Darden School of Business at UVA. Carol was a professor and an executive coach who helped John when he was the head of a financial firm in Charlotte. I set up a half-day session with her in Charlottesville, VA. When I met with her, I was beaten down, wondering if I was truly a poor leader as was written and said about me. I lacked confidence and walked into her beautiful home with my head down and shoulders slumped.

Carol had me take the Myers-Briggs assessment before our meeting, and she had researched my tenure at UNC. After some small talk, she gave me the results of my assessment, telling me I was an "ENTJ." I had been called a few four-letter words before, especially at places like Cameron Indoor Stadium and Reynolds Coliseum, but never an "ENTJ"! She explained what "ENTJ" meant and said only 2 percent of the population were "ENTJs." My head and shoulders lifted and my chest puffed out a little. It was the first time in weeks that I felt some pride. I thought, "I am elite! UNC just let go of an elite coach!" She probably sensed what I was feeling and quickly stated, "That means 98 percent of the population don't think like you think!"

Wow! I got it immediately. She went on to say that I was a "find the flaw" kind of coach. I looked for the mistakes instead of catching people doing things right. Message received!

The rest of the meeting was invigorating, as I was learning about a topic that I was never formally taught. Leadership!

Carol then invited me to take a leadership class at Darden that she taught with her husband, Jack. The only problem was the class cost $9,000! All the perks I had as the head coach were out the window. I had to recently spend $50,000 to buy my wife and myself cars. I had to buy a new cell phone. I had to put my house on the market. Now this! Fortunately, John Black, who was also a UNC booster, talked to Dick Baddour on my behalf and the athletic department paid for the class. For that, I was very grateful.

When a coach told me to work on something, like dribbling with my left hand, I was always determined to do it to the best of my ability. I always wanted to turn a weakness into a strength, and this was no different.

Studying leadership became my passion!

Not only did I take Carol's class at Darden, but I took a similar class at The Wharton School at Penn where my brother attended. I was also invited to take leadership classes from Dr. Jerry Bell in Chapel Hill. In addition, Dr. Bell conducted a

360 degree survey for me. That survey was given to all of my coaches and support staff at UNC. They filled out the extensive survey and Dr. Bell's staff put the comments in a typed document, protecting their identities.

I was at Darden for a week with business executives from across the country. We did a lot of reading and assignments. One case study was about a family-run company in Chicago where a new CEO came in from outside the organization to lead the business. The new CEO understood that he would be viewed as an outsider and how that would make the employees feel. He sat down with the employees and was slow to make any drastic changes. This comforted the employees. It showed respect to them and the former CEO, while gaining their trust. This foundation of respect and trust set him up, and the company, for success. He managed change appropriately.

As I sat in that class, it hit me, "Why don't we have formal leadership training in athletics?" If I had taken this class before I became a head coach, I might still be the coach at North Carolina. In college athletics, an assistant coach is often hired to lead a program and he is "given the keys to a Ferrari and told to drive as fast as you can, but don't wreck it." However, that coach is never given a lesson on how to drive a Ferrari!

At Wharton, we took several classes and toured Gettysburg where Abraham Lincoln gave his famous "Gettysburg Address." The class that impacted me the most was on emotional intelligence. I never heard of emotional intelligence until then! Fran Johnston was the instructor, and we were working out of the book *Primal Leadership: The Art of Emotional Intelligence* by Dan Goleman. Fran worked on that book with Dan and she ran the Teleos Leadership Institute in Philadelphia. As we were reading that first day, I saw a sentence that would change my life, "Leadership is a learned behavior." That line gave me hope, hope that I could, in fact, be a good leader. It was the most exciting thing I ever read.

After class, I went up to Fran and introduced myself. She knew of me and my background, and we became close friends. Fran invited me to work with her. She became my executive coach, and I would fly from Charlotte, where my family relocated, to Philadelphia once a month. I would fly up and back in a day for several months to meet with her and learn about leadership. It was exciting to learn and grow.

Fran once said, "You are a lifelong learner." I had never heard that term before, but it was a nice compliment and I realized that I was. I liked to learn and get better.

Dr. Bell had a seminar at The Carolina Inn in Chapel Hill, one of my favorite hotels. We learned a lot about communicating with others and how each person shares and receives information differently. In addition, Dr. Bell gave me the results of the 360 degree assessment. I was anxious to read it, as I would see the comments of my former staff members. There were some very critical comments, but as my friend Dr. Lanny Hass tells me, "You need to look at that as a gift." I did. I think is it imperative that leaders "mine for the truth." Many leaders are surrounded by people who are afraid to tell them the truth because they don't want to be scolded, reassigned, or fired. I often tell leaders now, "You are going to find out the truth sooner or later. You would rather know the truth now and manage it than to be holding a cardboard box with your personal belongings as you watch your car be driven down the street!"

By that time, we had relocated to Mooresville, NC. We felt we needed to leave Chapel Hill, but my wife and I wanted to stay in the state we loved. Kelly grew up in nearby Concord, so we were near her family and many good friends. About that time, I had another interesting experience at our church in town. We were attending the First Presbyterian Church, and the pastor of thirty plus years was retiring. That Sunday, they took the time to explain the process the church goes through in replacing the pastor. Their process is that the assistant pastor cannot become the head pastor, so they bring in an interim pastor who stays for a year. In addition, the retired pastor cannot have any official duties in the church. He can't conduct weddings or funerals. The interim pastor makes the necessary changes in preparation for the new permanent pastor and then the interim pastor moves on to his next interim position. This way, the new permanent pastor doesn't have to be the "bad guy" in making any unpopular changes that the membership may not like.

"Brilliant. What a concept!" I said to myself. Then I realized I was like an interim coach at UNC! I made drastic changes to the Carolina program upon my arrival that were not well received and I was considered the "bad guy." I changed some of the support staff, I brought my assistants with me, and we changed the appearance of the office and locker room. I made the changes that I believed were necessary to build a foundation of success. Unfortunately, I didn't get to reap any of the awards of my efforts.

CHAPTER NINETEEN:

THE BRIDGE OVER BITTER RIVER

"Moving on doesn't mean you forget about things,
it just means you have to accept what
happened and continue living."
—*Erza Scarlet*

"The Bridge" is a long winding road with a hefty emotional toll. There are many treacherous curves without guardrails. It was easy to drive off into the "Bitter River." Plus, the toll was so hefty I wasn't sure I wanted to even try to cross "The Bridge."

I was raised to say the right thing and have a good attitude … to be grateful. I remember Kelly quoting Sally Stanford, "When you are getting run out of town, get out in front of the crowd and make it look like a parade." We put up a good front in public. I was the former UNC coach. 2001 AP National Coach of the Year. I was "America's Guest." I'd play golf and was working for ESPN. We attended great events. Life wasn't too bad, as we moved into a new house, and were surrounded by family and good friends.

However, I drove into "The River" more than I care to admit! It didn't take much. Triggers were everywhere. A comment here, an article there, a game on TV ... I couldn't escape it. It wouldn't have mattered if I lived in California. These triggers were all over the place and they would drive me right into the water.

March was the toughest month for me because of the NCAA Tournament. Every year of my life since I was in fourth grade, I loved March Madness. Now it was just a huge trigger of negative emotions.

March 2005 may have been the worst month of my life. UNC was ripping through the NCAA Tournament and I was working for CSTV (now CBS College Sports) as a studio analyst in NYC. I loved the work, but with each Carolina win, I would drive off into "The River." That's my team! I recruited those guys! I rebuilt that program!

I wanted UNC to win. It was my alma mater. They were my players. But, part of me wanted them to lose. UNC didn't deserve to win after what they did to me and my family. "The River."

UNC marched all the way to the Final Four in St. Louis, and I had to cover it for CSTV. I had to say good things. I had to put up a strong front. It tore my insides up! It was harder on Kelly! Wives love their husbands and their kids even more. UNC threw her life and the lives of my kids into chaos.

Monday night, April 4, 2005, I watched the NCAA Championship game in the "Green Room" at CSTV Studios in Lower Manhattan. As I watched the game, I tried to stay on "The Bridge." The starting five of Sean May, Raymond Felton, Rashad McCants, Jawad Williams, and Jackie Manuel was the starting five I recruited to UNC. That was my starting lineup in 2003. I envisioned this moment, only with me coaching from the sidelines. My gut was turning. I wanted them to win. I wanted them to lose. Selfishly, if they won, I would get credit for recruiting the starting five that won the National Championship. If they lost, Carolina would get what they deserved.

Carolina won the game. The game was over, but I continued to sit in the "Green Room" as the other announcers were getting up to prepare to go on the air. They said, "Let's go." I told them, "I need a minute." I sat there watching each player climb the ladder and cut off a piece of the net. Finally, Roy was the last person up the ladder. He wore a National Championship hat as he cut the final strand. He turned to the crowd and pumped his fists in the air with the 2005 Championship net in his hand. My 2005 Championship net!

As I sat in a daze, my phone rang. It was former UVA coach Terry Holland. He told me that he was thinking of me at this time and that he knew it had to be hard to watch, but I should be proud of that team. Coach Holland had recruited me. I played against his teams. He was our AD at Davidson. We have become good friends since I left UNC. He is all class!

During my time in TV, I felt the itch to coach again. I was too young, and I didn't want UNC to be my last job. One day driving home on Brawley School Road in Mooresville, my phone rang. It was Ryan Humphrey! He finished a great career at Notre Dame and was playing professionally. He was just checking on me. Here was a young man I recruited to Notre Dame, and then I left him after one year. He was calling me to see how I was doing! He is truly an amazing person. After some small talk, he said, "You're a good coach. You need to be coaching!"

I had looked at various coaching jobs in 2003 and 2004. Several places wouldn't even talk to me! The damage to my reputation after UNC was too much for some athletic directors to overcome. In 2004, I was offered the James Madison job and was prepared to take it, but St. John's came calling. It was the Big East. It was home. My sister Nan attended SJU. My niece, Maura, went there. I was connected there. I met with several people involved in the search in Jim Reilly's Park Avenue apartment in NYC. Jim knew my family from "The Park" where he was a lifeguard with my sisters in the 1970s and he was a big St. John's booster. He wanted me to have the job, but as I sat in his beautiful apartment, the other men grilled me about my time at UNC. The questions were about dealing with players and how I would manage the team. They asked a lot of questions about why I was forced to resign. I felt I was being interrogated. After a long period of uncomfortable questions, one man asked about style of play. "Finally," I said as we got to discussing basketball! I felt I overcame the "elephant in the room."

After passing the first test, I was invited back to meet with President Father Harrington and the athletic director at the Ritz-Carlton in Lower Manhattan. Kelly joined me. We talked and had lunch in a large suite. The visit was going great. We were all very comfortable. After lunch, President Harrington asked me, "What will it take for you to be our next coach?" I put my hand on his shoulder and said, "Seven years at one million per year." He said, "Okay. Can you do a press conference next week?" I said, "Yes, but James Madison offered me their head coaching position and I told them I would respond today. Should I call them and tell them 'no'?" I was asking to confirm that my being the next SJU coach was a done deal. He said, "Yes." I went into the hallway and called JMU's AD Jeff Bourne and turned down the job. I was excited. NYC. Family. Madison Square Garden. The Big East. I was back!

Kelly and I flew home to Charlotte, and I quickly turned around and went to the Final Four in San Antonio. My mind raced about being back in NYC. Who would be on staff? Recruiting? Where would we live? I remember trying to reach the St. John's athletic director several times. No answer. Weird. We were going to have a press conference in a few days! I finally connected with him. His mood was somber. He finally said, "We are going in a different direction." What!

Rumor had it that Lou Carnesecca didn't want me at St. John's. Coach Carnesecca was an iconic figure there. He tried to recruit me to St. John's, but I didn't show any interest. He didn't want a Carolina guy coaching his program.

I turned down a good Division I job for St. John's in front of President Father Harrington and now I don't have anywhere to coach!

After another year of TV, I felt I had to coach again because if I stayed out too long, I may never get another shot. In the spring of 2005, there weren't great options. Craig Angelos called me asking about coaching candidates for the coaching position at Florida Atlantic University in Boca Raton, FL. Craig was the athletic director. He ran a few names by me and I gave him my thoughts. Finally, I said, "I might be interested." He was surprised, but I needed a place to coach. I ended up getting the job. It was exciting to be wanted again.

My family and I attended the press conference with Rex Walters. He was going to be on my staff. After the press conference, my family flew home, and Rex and I immediately went to work. We had a lot to do. We walked into our humble office and I went to my desk. I sat down and pulled out the drawer to find a pen. With that, the whole drawer came out onto my lap. Pens and pencils flew all over the floor. In frustration, I looked out the window and got upset. I thought, "Just two years ago,

I was the head coach at North Carolina. I had a big office and flew on private planes. Now I am at a low Division I program with a broken desk!" My career had hit the bottom.

I drove off "The Bridge" into the "Bitter River." I got mad at UNC all over again. They did this to me. They damaged my career to the point of having to take a job where my desk doesn't even work! That night, I went to my hotel room and laid in bed, depressed. What did I just do? Why did I take this job? Why am I in this position? What am doing to my family? For the previous two years, we had a nice life living in Mooresville. We had a nice house. I enjoyed doing TV. Now this!

There were many days that summer I thought about quitting. My family was still in NC. I lived in a nice apartment overlooking the beach until we bought a house, but I was depressed. I struggled to get out of bed. I remember going to recruit at a camp in New Jersey. I pulled up in front of the campus and just stayed in my car. I didn't want to get out. I tried to go to sleep. I WAS depressed.

I talked to my wife about quitting. She quickly said, "You can't do that to your assistants!" How about that! She didn't want to be there. She loved her new house in North Carolina. She was near her family and childhood friends and our kids were settled. But Kelly Propst Doherty is tough and as loyal as the day is long. She set me straight.

It turned out to be a rewarding year. We had a good season. We made a difference. Then SMU called and we moved to Dallas, TX. I loved the campus and we loved living in University Park. It was a great place to raise Tucker and Hattie, and we made lifelong friends.

But triggers continued to surface. I was at the Peach Jam in Georgia on a recruiting trip. It was a big event and every top player east of the Mississippi was there. As a result, every major program was there to recruit. I found myself sitting next to UNC assistant coach Steve Robinson. Steve and I worked for Roy at Kansas. I was close to Steve, even though he would kick my butt in racquetball all the time! As we talked, I brought up my time at UNC and how I felt about my ouster and Roy taking over. I shared with him my feelings about some of things I was upset about in the transition. Things that were said and things that weren't said. Things that were done and things that weren't done. I was hurting. My tone turned intense.

I drove right off "The Bridge" into the "Bitter River!"

It's easy to swerve off the road and become bitter. Staying on the road to become better is hard! It is a long-term process. It will test even the best of men and women.

CHAPTER TWENTY:

FORGIVENESS

"Father, forgive them, for they know not what they do."
—LUKE 23:34 ESV

I struggled for years with the pain of being forced to resign at my alma mater. Why did it happen? Should I have stayed at Notre Dame? Why did they publicly shame me? I was depressed, really depressed. I talked with doctors and psychologists and took medication. I kept that private because I didn't want people to see me broken. But I was! I had a difficult time sleeping. I would often dream of coaching UNC or conversations I might have with Dean Smith and Roy Williams.

I remember talking to Fran Johnston on one of my trips to Philadelphia. As I struggled with moving on from UNC, I tried to justify it by saying, "People are forced to resign in business all the time!" As if that was going to make me feel better. Men, especially athletes and coaches, are supposed to be tough! Fran responded, "But you trusted these men since you were seventeen years old. They were like father figures to you." She was right! Fran helped me understand and justify the pain I was trying to work through.

I tried to set up a meeting with Coach Smith several times. I knew I had to have a face-to-face visit about all that happened during my time as UNC's coach. I needed closure, but it was hard to make that call. I often picked up the phone to call him and then stopped. Unfortunately, we never got to have that meeting. By the time I got to set up a meeting with Roy Williams, Coach Smith was already suffering with his health and wasn't able to participate.

The meeting was scheduled in Coach Williams' office. For six long years, I mentally prepared for that meeting. I played the conversations over and over again in my head. I wanted to come across professionally and, most importantly, as a strong man! There was a lot I needed to get off my mind. Finally, we both sat down in Roy's office. It was the same office I occupied six years prior! It was surreal. I could tell Roy was anxious, as was I. As I started to talk, I immediately got choked up. Then I started to get emotional and I couldn't control it! I must have cried for a minute straight. I was mad at myself for allowing my emotions to get the best of me. I wanted to be tough and in control, but I couldn't manage the feelings flowing out of my soul.

After I gathered myself, I told Roy all the issues and concerns I had during my time as coach and in the transition from my tenure to his. There were many things that I didn't feel were "right." I needed to let him know how it made me feel. Roy was good. He listened. He was patient. When I left that meeting, it felt like six hundred pounds were lifted off my shoulders. For the first time in six years, I had a good night's sleep!

Meeting with Roy was a big challenge, but the biggest challenge in the whole process was forgiveness. I had to learn to forgive others. They were "renting space" in my head and my soul. Selfishly, forgiveness is the best thing one can do because it is freeing. If Jesus could forgive the men who crucified him, I could forgive people that I felt may have wronged me.

In addition, I needed to forgive myself! Forgiving yourself is very difficult. I always strived to be perfect! As a result, when I make a mistake, I am extremely hard on myself. I replay events over and over in my mind, wondering what I could have done differently. Plus, there were so many triggers that would get my mind racing down a destructive path. Triggers such as UNC playing on TV, Roy winning the National Championship in 2005, Raymond Felton playing in the NBA, Notre Dame playing on TV, Mike Brey signing an extension at Notre Dame, and a coach getting fired with a huge buyout … I couldn't run from these triggers. So I needed to, I HAD to, forgive myself in order to find peace.

Finally, I got down on my knees and prayed. I wanted to open my heart to forgive those who I felt may have wronged me. In addition, I prayed for forgiveness for myself. I finally felt a peace come over me. A peace that I hadn't experienced in a long time.

I still struggle. March is very difficult for me as I see head coaches leading their teams in the magical moments of March Madness. I struggle seeing my contemporaries having success coaching in college and in the NBA. I often ask, "Why me?"

Fortunately, many of the Carolina faithful are very kind to me. People thank me for my time as a player and a coach and for recruiting a team that won the NCAA Championship in 2005. Roy and his staff are very welcoming when I have gone back to Chapel Hill for a game or to watch practice when I worked for the Indiana Pacers. Roy even had a picture of me along with former UNC coaches Frank McGuire, Dean Smith and Bill Guthridge on the wall of the coaches' locker room. Having Bubba Cunningham as the AD at UNC has made things easier, too. He has been a good friend for a long time, even though he was going to penalize me two strokes when I asked him if I could move my ball out a fairway divot in 2000!

My daughter even got to attend UNC. Hattie entered school there in 2007 as a rower. She has blossomed into a great young lady at Carolina. I am very proud of the fact that she, too, is a Tar Heel!

All in all, I am proud of my time as a player and coach at UNC and all the other programs I coached at. I believe my staff and I left those programs in position for success.

I'm Matt Doherty and I am a Tar Heel!

THE FINAL CHAPTER:

GROWTH ZONE

"I never lose. I either win or learn."
—Nelson Mandela

I learned a lot of lessons looking back on my painful experience as the head coach at North Carolina. I was fortunate to learn from the classes I took at Darden and Wharton, along with the great executive coaches I met along the way—Carol and Jack Weber, Dr. Jerry Bell, and Fran Johnston. These lessons are formatted in a way that I hope you find useful as a reference for your personal growth. We all lead in some manner, whether it be as a parent, in business, in academia, in church, or in your community. Now more than ever, we need good leadership in our country.

Learn and Grow!

CORE VALUES

Core values are critical, as they drive behavior. At UNC, Dean Smith instilled the mantra of Play Hard, Play Smart,

Play Together. These core values are still a pillar of Carolina basketball today!

My core values are RTCP: Respect, Trust, Commitment, and Positivity. Respect is the most important value. Every human being wants to feel respected. Without respect, no other value can take root. Trust is critical for a company to fully blossom. If you have a trusting culture, you will be amazed at what your organization will be able to accomplish. Without trust there will be dysfunction. Commitment to the vision, your people, and your role in the organization. Everyone needs to feel the commitment to a common cause to achieve lofty goals. Positive energy makes work fun and helps organizations blow through obstacles.

Core values need to be three to four words that can be easily remembered. Why are phone numbers three to four digits long? Because it is easier to remember three or four things than seven.

Core values need to guide every decision. Live it. Model it.

When I got to SMU in 2006, I instilled the core values of RTC (I didn't add "P" until 2020). I discussed the values of respect, trust, and commitment in our first team meeting. In that meeting, I had a shoebox-sized limestone with a gold plate on it. The gold plate read "SMU Basketball 2006-07 RTC." This stone was going to be the foundation of our program. I asked the players and coaches to sign the stone with a Sharpie. It was a "contract" to uphold these values. In addition, I gave them medallions and rubber wrist bands with "RTC" on them. The medallion idea came from the challenge coin Lt. Colonel Matt Karres had given me years prior.

Mandatory class attendance was a requirement of any team I coached. One day, I learned that a player was not attending class, so I called him into my conference room before practice. He sat across from me. I was quiet. No small talk. In the middle of the conference table sat the stone with our core values and everyone's signature on it. I started calmly, "I hear you aren't attending class?" His head dropped. I asked, "Is it true?" He meekly responded, "Yes." I then pointed to the stone and asked, "Did you sign this stone?" He meekly responded again, "Yes." Remaining calm, I stated, "Since you signed the stone to uphold the program's core values of Respect, Trust, and Commitment and you are skipping class, you have broken each of these values. One, you are not respecting the rule of mandatory class attendance. Two, you broke a trust with me because I thought you were attending class. And three, you are showing a lack of commitment toward your education." I paused for effect. I wanted it to sink in. I proceeded by asking him, "If you were me, what would you do?" After a few seconds he responded, "I would suspend me." I quickly said, "Okay. You're suspended." We got up and walked out the door to practice. No yelling. No hard feelings. Message received. And more importantly, I knew he would go into the locker room with all his teammates eager to hear what happened. I trust that his response to his teammates went something like this, "Coach found out I was skipping class, but he was cool. We discussed how I broke our core values, and now I am suspended. But, I kind of suspended myself!"

That was one of my proudest coaching moments!

MISSION STATEMENT

Every good organization has a GOOD mission statement. It is the rudder that steers the ship. Every big decision should be made with the mission statement in mind. Mission statements must be a clear and concise statements that can be easily remembered. They must be impactful.

My mission statement is to "Make a positive impact on the people I meet and the groups I work with." Simple. Memorable. Impactful.

I do a lot of corporate speaking engagements and I love to ask, "What is your company's mission statement?" Most people start talking, then look up in the air and offer an awkward giggle as they shrug their shoulders. Other people say, "Hold on a second" and pull out a sheet of paper and start reading a long paragraph as my eyes start to glaze over.

If your team doesn't know your mission statement off the top of their heads, it's a problem. Mission statements are a living, breathing statement that should drive your organization.

S.T.E.V.I.T. — THE SIX KNOWS OF LEADERSHIP

I often use acronyms to help me remember things. It helped me get through college and teach my players the keys on our scouting reports. By making up a story about "this guy STEVIT I recruited from Wisconsin…" I can remember my "Six Knows of Leadership"—S.T.E.V.I.T— Self, Team, Environment, Vision, Industry, and the Truth.

I believe these are six pillars to becoming a successful leader:

1. SELF

You must understand your blind spots. Everyone has strengths and weaknesses. Your biggest strength is also your biggest weakness.

I am a literal person. When someone tells me something, I take it for its face value. For example, when Coach Smith told me, "It's your program, run it how you see fit," I believed it. Every word. But, I learned that you need to read body language and the tone of people when they talk and understand their motives.

Respect is a HUGE trigger for me. I am an intense and competitive person. These traits were ingrained in me at an early age playing basketball at The Park. The only way to survive there was to be intense and competitive. This got you respect. When Duke's Chris Collins came onto the court in our game in Chapel Hill and challenged me, I went after him.

The key for me is keeping things in an "emotional circle." My intensity and competitiveness are good things. . . in moderation, but once I go outside the "emotional circle," there can be collateral damage that leads to "coaching scars."

When I coached at FAU, Rex Walters was my assistant. I coached Rex at Kansas, and he is like a brother to me. At FAU, I told Rex that if I grabbed the bridge of my nose at practice and started to walk to the opposite end of the court, he was to take over. I put myself in "time-out" to calm down so I wouldn't "spew mercury" at the team and create a "coaching scar."

"Spewing mercury" is when you feel the mercury rise from your stomach through your esophagus into your mouth and out at your team.

If you don't know yourself, how can you lead others? I suggest everyone take the DISC and/or Myers-Briggs assessments. They are invaluable tools.

2. TEAM

As with yourself, your team has their strengths and weaknesses. You need to put them in position to be successful, where they complement each other to create the most productive team possible. Each team has a collective personality, and there are individual personalities.

Not everyone is wired the same. Study your players and have "real" conversations with your team. Spend uninterrupted time where you can get them to share their dreams, fears, and motivations. This builds trust and allows you to know what "buttons" to push and, more importantly, what "buttons" not to push.

At Notre Dame, I could really get on the team and they would respond. They became a mentally tough team. However, with some individuals, I felt it was better to coax. Martin Ingelsby started the year before I got there. He was a great shooter and smart player. Currently, he is doing a great job as the head coach at Delaware. I wanted Martin to set harder screens. I felt yelling at Martin wouldn't be an effective way to communicate, so I started calling him "Stockton." As I mentioned earlier, John Stockton was a great player in the NBA. He was known for his toughness and willingness to set hard screens on the biggest centers he faced. The more I called Martin "Stockton," the better screens he set.

3. ENVIRONMENT

Where are the "land mines" you need to avoid? Former employees? Legacy leaders? A disgruntled person who didn't get the job? Politics are real! Understand where the power lies.

Looking back at North Carolina, I should have asked Coach Smith about bringing my staff with me. He was the most influential person in the process. Even though Dick Baddour had the title of athletic director, that didn't mean he was the only one who had power over me.

When I got to SMU, there was a professor who loved basketball. He would attend a lot of high school games in Dallas and became close to the high school coaches. When I saw him on campus, he was always cordial, but I got word that he was saying a lot of bad things about SMU in the community. Obviously, I was concerned how this might impact recruiting. I had a decision to make. Was I going to continue to be cordial and act like nothing was going on or would I confront him? Well, since I am intense and competitive, I confronted him, but it was important to do it in a respectful manner. I saw him at a high school event in the city and went up to him and asked, "Why are you saying bad things about SMU in the community? You work at SMU. SMU is a great school, and we need you to be an ambassador for the program." Like most people, he was uncomfortable with someone confronting him. He denied my accusations, but I never had a problem with him again!

I believe in having "crucial conversations" to put everything on the table.

4. VISION

Where do you want to go as an organization and how are you going to get there? This needs to be communicated to your team on a regular basis. It is a great tool for motivating people.

When I got to Notre Dame, I talked about bringing the glory days back to South Bend. Digger Phelps had elevated the program to the national spotlight in the 1970s and 1980s. I wanted to bring that back. I painted a visual picture of what that looked like. Packed arenas. Huge victories. Fans storming the courts. Big East titles. National Championships. Then I would ask the players, "Don't you want that?" Everyone would nod in acceptance. That was the hook. Now I had them. This excited them to practice hard and compete. And when they didn't, I would say, "Remember that time in the locker room when we talked about winning big games and championships? Well, it takes hard work, and we are not working hard."

5. INDUSTRY

It is paramount that you continue to "Learn and Grow." Knowing your industry and the future trends is critical for any leader. You need to be the industry expert. It will give your team the confidence that they are following a competent leader. People want to win. Give them that chance.

I loved scouting, going to clinics, and visiting with coaches. I wanted to learn and get better.

One of my greatest thrills was meeting with Coach Smith one-on-one to talk basketball. I had the greatest basketball coach of all time at my disposal. He would often attend practice and sit up in a luxury box, out of sight. I could look up there and see only his head in the dark box. The next day, we would meet in the coaches' locker room, he would give me a page or two of notes, and we would go over them. Wow! What an experience for this young head coach.

I remember asking him a question every coach struggles with today, "If you are up three points with seven seconds to play and the other team had the ball, do you foul?" He responded, "Coach McGuire would say, 'You have to do what the fans will understand.'" I smiled ear to ear. Here was a living legend quoting Frank McGuire, the coach who won the 1957 NCAA Championship at UNC. The coach who hired Dean Smith to come to Chapel Hill as his assistant. I felt tremendous pride that I was getting linked all the way back to Coach McGuire.

6. TRUTH

It is imperative to "mine for the truth." You must have at least one person on your staff who is a "truth teller." A person who can close the door and give you straight talk. They should be able to tell you the truth about team morale and the feelings of the players and staff about decisions, roles, or processes.

You need to create a "safe zone" in staff meetings so people willingly share their ideas without getting ridiculed for their comments. When someone disagrees with you, you need to say, "That is a great idea. I really appreciate you bringing that up." This will create an environment that fosters new and innovative ideas and makes you and the organization better. Plus, it follows the core values of RTCP. Showing respect to your staff, creating trust that you won't bully them, and a commitment to them and the program's success all done in a positive manner. I have been around several bosses who bully people when a suggestion is made because it is counter to theirs. Do you think anyone else will offer an opinion after that? It stifles creativity and it is utterly disrespectful.

One tactic I learned reading a leadership book was about staff meetings. It suggested that you ask the most junior person on your staff first when getting an opinion about a decision the leader was going to make. The reasoning is that the most junior person may have the best idea, but if you go in the opposite order and ask him or her last, they may defer to the others out of respect or fear.

At UNC, I remember many meetings in my office where I would ask David Cason his opinion first. He was our director of operations and the youngest person on staff. But David was smart and had a great feel of the players because he was around them the most. He would often share some wisdom that we may never have received had he been asked last.

Eventually, the truth will surface, and you don't want to be the last person to find out! "If you don't manage the truth, the truth will manage you!"

SERVANT LEADERSHIP

As a leader, you have to sacrifice. You give yourself up to others. You and your spouse need to understand this. Your time isn't your own. It is a full-time commitment. All the stakeholders—fans, the community, and your industry—need to see you, touch you, and hear your voice. A leader can't hide from this responsibility; otherwise, you are not leading. It takes a great deal of energy, but it is what you sign up for when you accept a leadership position.

Invest in your people. They are your most precious resource. Help them grow individually. Training is essential for stimulation and growth of your staff. This not only helps them, but it will make your organization stronger, while creating a level of gratitude that will help develop a loyalty that you want your people to have for you and the organization.

Meet with your staff and ask how you can make their position better for them. Ask for their input. If they have reasonable requests, do your best to fulfill them. This shows respect, develops trust, and shows commitment.

There was no better servant leader than Dean Smith. That is why all his former players and staff were so loyal to him. He would meet with every senior after they were done playing to plan for their futures. He helped so many former players get jobs. He would write all the former players handwritten notes each year. He loved his players. He was proud of his players. He always put his players first.

When we had pre-game meals, the players got their food before the coaches. When we traveled, the upperclassmen flew first class and the coaches sat in coach. When the team won, he praised the players. When the team lost, he blamed himself. The list goes on and on and on.

But the most amazing thing he did was after he passed away. About two months after Coach died, I came home and there was an envelope on the kitchen counter. I opened it up and there was a letter from Coach. The letter thanked me for my time as a player and it said to take my family out to dinner on him, and there was a $200 check included! Simply amazing!

MODEL

Model the behavior you want from your team. If you don't model it, but you demand it, you are a fraud! "RTCP." Showing respect, clean up after yourself, show up on time, give people your full attention, follow up in a timely manner, etc.

Consistency is critical, as once people witness you doing something wrong, it will stand out more than when you do something right. Your mood needs to be consistent, too. Leaders who are up and down emotionally create an atmosphere of uneasiness that will inhibit overall production and reduce trust. Temperament is such an important part of leadership. The ability to stay calm in the face of adversity is a challenge for many of us, but it can be developed.

Dean Smith NEVER cursed. That is a statistic that is more impressive than his all-time wins record. With all the stressful situations he faced, he never once cursed. Not even on the golf course!

I wish I could be more like Coach!

Being on time was important to Coach Smith, Coach Williams, Bob McKillop, and me. My first game at Notre Dame was at Ohio State. After pre-game meal, everyone would go back to their rooms and rest before getting on the bus and heading over to the arena. Since we were staying only a couple of miles away, we told the team, "The bus is LEAVING at 5:30

p.m." We got on the bus. It was 5:30 p.m. We left. On the short ride over, there was a lot of traffic. As we sat in traffic, I see this man dressed in all black walking over the small bridge, carrying a duffle bag. It was our priest!

NUGGETS:

- "Start how you finish." —Dean Smith.

- "If you are late, you are telling others that your time is more important than theirs." —Dean Smith

- "People don't like moody!"

- "Actions speak louder than words!"

ORGANIZATION

Put systems in place to ensure that your organization is run as efficiently as possible. Learn from others who have run successful organizations.

Have a daily plan. This guards against slippage and distractions. Prioritize your time because it is such a valuable resource that can't be wasted. Write down your most important daily tasks and check them off. Simple, but effective.

Plan weekly staff meetings with agendas so your staff knows how to prepare.

When I was an assistant coach at Davidson, I tried to be extremely organized. I believe you "control what you can control." I was always trying to find the best way to do things, and I came across the Franklin Planner. It is a daily planner that helps you prioritize your day, your month, your year, and your life. I became obsessed with it. I have tried to find better options, even with all the new technology today, but there is nothing better than writing down notes and prioritizing your day on paper. I still carry one.

Every assistant coach I had, I made them use a Franklin Planner and would challenge them to find a better option. Mike Balado was an assistant for me at FAU. He had great energy, was a good recruiter, and knew basketball, but he wasn't the most organized person I knew! Mike is now the head coach at Arkansas State, and he still uses the Franklin Planner. His beautiful wife, Alicia, once thanked me for making him more organized.

NUGGETS:

- "You either manage your day or your day will manage you."

- "If you fail to plan, you are planning to fail." —Ben Franklin

- "Little things are big things." —Bob McKillop

- "If you take care of the little things, the big things take care of themselves." —Emily Dickinson

- "Time is your biggest opponent. Choose your tasks wisely."

- "Paper remembers. People forget." —NYC pizzeria owner

- Eliminate distractions—cell phones, emails, and social media eat at productivity.

- Delegate—if someone can do a project 80 percent as well as you can, let them manage it. This develops trust and it is the best way for your people to grow while taking stress off yourself.

- "Don't mistake activity with achievement." — John Wooden

- Learn to say "no."

- "Gatekeepers" should manage your requests. You don't want to be the "bad guy."

- Deadlines—agree upon deadlines with your staff, then track the progress. Hold people accountable.

- Flowcharts—do you have a chain of command?

STRATEGY

I wrote about core values, mission statements, and vision. Now you have to have a strategy.

The questions you must ask are, "What do we have to do to be successful? Who do we have to beat? What is the best strategy to accomplish this?"

At UNC, for us to be successful, we had to beat Duke. We had to develop a strategy to beat one of the best coaches in all of basketball. To do that, we had to recruit great players and put them in position to beat Duke. We had to know as much as possible about Duke. Their university. Their student body. The way they recruited. Who they were recruiting? Their style of play. Their key plays. The list goes on.

When we were getting ready to play Duke in my first matchup as head coach at UNC, assistant coach Doug Wojcik found out that Duke was going to trap the ball when our center inbounded after made free throws. We always had our big men inbound the ball in those situations. Since our big men weren't great dribblers in the open court, I didn't want to put them in position to turn the ball over. In our practice, we decided to have guard Joe Forte inbound the ball on made FTs so when the trap came, we threw it back to Joe and he would race the ball up the court and attack the defense, creating a four-on-three situation. It worked and it forced Duke to change their strategy.

We turned Duke's strength into a weakness.

I believe you have to have a "What if?" mentality. What if your best player gets hurt? What if we are behind twenty points with ten minutes to go? What if a key employee leaves? What if it snows? What if there is traffic on the way to the airport?

Dean Smith was a master at this. He told me to have a play that will work against a man-to-man defense or a zone so when you call time-out at the end of the game you won't be surprised with a change in the defense. Brilliant. I took his advice after that. On the flip side, when a team called a time-out at the end of the game to set up a play, oftentimes I would change my defense.

CULTURE

"Culture eats strategy for breakfast."
—Peter Drucker

Culture is hard to define, but easy to feel. It is the accumulation of many things shared in this book. If you get all of the above right, the culture of your organization will take shape.

One of the reasons I added the "P," positivity, to my core values of RTCP is because I hated being around negative people. Long-time college coach and good friend Kevin Stallings once told me, "There are two types of players—energy givers and energy suckers." I call energy suckers "termites" because they eat at the foundation of your organization. No one likes being around them. "Termites" come in the form of ego, jealousy, insecurity, and negativity. Your culture must create an environment where ego and jealousy are avoided at all costs. "Team Ego > Individual Ego." In an environment with individual ego and jealousy, people will not share information, and as a result, the organization will not reach its maximum potential.

One of my favorite leadership books was *Jack: Straight from the Gut* by Jack Welch. He was the CEO of General Electric. He shared "The Four Es" listed below. I used this with my teams and in scouting for the Indiana Pacers. If a player had "The Four Es," he could play for me!

THE FOUR Es (JACK WELCH):

1. **Energy** — hire people who bring energy to the workplace. Energy is needed to overcome daily obstacles and it creates a stimulating work environment.

2. **Energize** — inevitably, people will have down days. This is when your teammates need to be able to energize each other to raise their games to attack the day.

3. **Execute** — an organization needs people who can execute. Doers. Get the job done!

4. **Edge** — in a competitive business, you need people who can execute with an edge. Sometimes, you will have to make tough choices that may not be popular with others. Sometimes, you have to challenge the status quo. Sometimes, you will need to cut down the competition and "throw an elbow."

When I look at "The Four Es" and I think about basketball, I think of Michael Jordan. No one had the energy he did. No one could energize his team like he could. No one could execute like him. And no one, I mean no one, had the edge he had! "The Four Es" were the keys to his greatness.

Donnie Walsh is a longtime NBA executive and former player at UNC. He worked for the Pacers, and I would try to sit with him on the bench while the players were out on the court early before games. He once said to me, "You know, Matt. After all these years in the NBA, I think the most important thing in a player is energy."

NUGGETS:

- TEAM = Together Everyone Achieves More!

- People working as one will create an organization where "the whole is greater than the sum of its parts."

- "1+1=3 when 2 work as 1!"

DECISIONS

*"Put a picture of your family on your desk.
This will be a reminder that every decision
you make should be in their best interest."*
—JOHN BLACK

When I was at SMU, I felt the need to fire an assistant coach. It was the first time I was going to do this. It was a burden that I wrestled with for a while. I could be a nice guy and keep the status quo or I could make the difficult decision and let him go. I finally committed to letting him go when I looked at the picture of my family on my desk and asked, "Is this coach able to help me take care of my family?" The answer was easy. It was "no." After consulting with human resources, I met with him and told him I was letting him go. Like most cases, there was pushback, and as I listened, I kept thinking of my family and stood my ground. He wasn't going to help me provide for my family. He wasn't going to add enough value to my program that I would be able to keep my job. It made it easier to execute the tough decisions all leaders face.

Create a "Personal Board of Directors" who can help you with big decisions. I learned this from Bob Beaudine of Dallas where he runs an executive search firm. You need to have people who aren't emotionally involved in your decision. That way, you can get clarity of the pros and cons of your options.

When I was coaching, my PBOD was Dean Smith and Roy Williams. Every career decision I made, I discussed with them. When I was working for Roy at Kansas, I had several opportunities to take a head coaching job. Working for him attracted a lot of great opportunities. I interviewed for a few jobs and he prepared me well for those interviews, but afterward, he would say, "I don't think that is the right job for you." So I turned them down. Simple as that. After seven years on his staff, I was starting to wonder if I would get a good job. St. Louis had opened up and I didn't even get an interview. It was a good job and I had recruited one of the best players from that area, Ryan Robertson. One year later, I was the head coach at Notre Dame!

Have protocols. Dean Smith prioritized his time in this order: 1. Current players, 2. Recruits, and 3. Former players. If a former player was on the phone with Coach and a recruit called to talk with him, he would have to hang up and talk with the recruit. Subsequently, if a player walked in and had to talk with Coach while he was on the phone with a recruit, Coach would drop what he was doing to visit with the current player. Everyone knew of this protocol. It showed tremendous respect to the people who were most important to the organization and in the order of importance.

There are crucial decisions that you need to make to be successful and there are secondary decisions that aren't necessary to make right away. Decide what absolutely needs to be done in the short term and let the other decisions sit on the "back burner" to be addressed at a later date. Pick your battles and understand the political ramifications.

How do you slow down and clear your mind in pressure situations? Find a quiet place and lean on your Board of Directors.

Don't trick yourself into thinking there is "a sign" that you should make a certain decision. That is too easy and often reckless. I remember walking through Walmart in South Bend while I was deciding about taking the UNC job or not. I saw someone wearing a UNC sweatshirt and thought it was "a sign" that I should take the job! That was ridiculous, but your mind will play tricks on you under stress.

Take as much time as possible to think through the potential outcomes that will come from critical decisions. What are the unintended consequences? When I made decisions to move the season ticket holders' seats, I should have taken the time to think through the collateral damage that would occur. I should have asked more questions. I should have slowed down.

NUGGETS:

- "A good plan violently executed right now is far better than a perfect plan executed next week." — General Patton

- Pick your battles and understand the political ramifications. You don't have to win every battle.

- Having great options is sometimes a burden.

- Everyone is selling something. A player wants more playing time. An employee wants a promotion. A recruiter wants to hire you. People often tell you what they think you want to hear. Do your best to understand the motives behind the people.

- Weigh the best-case scenario and the worst-case scenario. If you can live with the worst-case scenario and the upside to the new position is greater than your present situation, you should make the move.

- Core values and mission statements are key to making decisions. These are the rudder that will keep your ship sailing in the right direction when you are faced with the rough seas of leadership.

COMMUNICATION

"Listening is a talent."
–MATT DOHERTY

Aggressively listen. Listening is a skill that needs constant attention because it can easily deteriorate.

Create an environment removed from distractions. Have a sitting area away from your desk where there are no barriers between you and the person you are visiting with. Open space leads to open conversation. Make sure you hide your cell phone, close your computer, and don't look at your watch. I always had a clock strategically placed in my office that I could glance at during private meetings. In addition, I would notify my secretary to interrupt me with an "important call" after a designated amount of time to excuse me from the meeting.

Mirror the other person's body language. This breaks down any "walls" that may exist. Repeat statements. This shows the other person that you are actively listening and it forces you to stay in the moment, keeping your mind locked in. Take notes. This lets the other person know that their comments really matter.

$E + R = O$. Tim Kight is a leadership coach and is a good follow on Twitter. He teaches this formula, $E + R = O$. E = the event. R = your reaction. O = the outcome. You can't control the event, but you control how you react to it. The better you react, the better the outcome. React slowly!

I took my family on vacation to Niagara Falls one summer. As we were looking over the railing at the power waterfall, someone stepped in front of me, blocking my view. I started to lean forward to "box him out," but I backed away. My daughter leaned into my ear and said, "Good R, Dad!"

"Coaching scars" is what Bob McKillop calls them, and all leaders have them. Moments when they react too fast and say something that cuts to the core. These comments will have long-lasting implications that leaders will wish they could get back. I wish I never approached Sean about calling Lubbock!

My good friend Scott Stankavage played football at UNC while I was in school. I asked him to read the manuscript for *Rebound*. He shared this wisdom with me:

INTENTION VS. INTERPRETATION FROM SCOTT STANKAVAGE:

A. Intention is singular. One person's intentions have a huge impact on others.

B. Our intention is what WE think it is.

C. Interpretation is for the masses.

D. Interpretation has a life span. People, those involved or not involved, bystanders, and pundits are in charge of the interpretation.

E. "Interpretation is the variable we control the least, but we should be concerned with the most." — Scott Stankavage

NUGGETS:

- Dr. Bell states that, "50 percent of communication is body language, 35 percent is tone, and 15 percent is content." It's not what you say, but how you say it.

- "The single biggest problem in communication is the illusion that it has taken place." —George Bernard Shaw

- "Effective communication values the recipient over the sender." —Neil Gordon

- "Great generals do not give commands that can be understood. They give commands that cannot be misunderstood." —General Douglas MacArthur

- "No man has listened himself out of a job." —Calvin Coolidge

HIRE RIGHT

"It is easy to hire, hard to fire."
–Matt Doherty

First of all, when taking over a new organization, you need to give your employees a clean slate. They may just need a fresh start. You would hate to overlook some gems. Wouldn't you want to be treated that way? If I listened to other people, Jimmy Dillon and Karen Wesolek wouldn't have been given the chance to make such a great impact for me at Notre Dame.

You must bring the right people into your organization. They must fit your core values and culture. This takes a lot of time and effort. Do your research, gathering key intel. Have your staff interview them so they are included in this critical process. This shows your staff respect. They need to feel good that this candidate can add value to the team. Trust and respect their input.

Define roles in the hiring process and hold people accountable for the execution of their roles. Set expectations in terms of bonuses, perks, and promotions. Let them know if you think there is a chance that you could bring in someone in the future who may be higher on the organizational chart than them.

When I was interviewing assistants at Notre Dame, I had Doug Wojcik meet with the candidates. After meeting with one coach, he came into my office and said, "I don't like him. He is cocky. I don't think he's a good fit." Done. That candidate was crossed off the list.

"Circle of trust." Hire people you know. If you look to hire someone you don't know well, someone you know well must know them well. As mentioned earlier, everyone I hired at Notre Dame, I personally knew or someone I knew VERY well knew that person well. The mistakes I made in hiring staff occurred when I went beyond my "circle of trust."

Augment. Make sure your staff augments your skill set and complements each other. This gives your staff great range to cover a multitude of areas—planning, budgeting, technical skills, sales, accounting, and communicative skills.

Bringing in people from outside the institution can be good because they help change the status quo. Just because it has been done a certain way for a long time doesn't mean it's the right way. When I was at SMU, I wanted to change our style of play to the "Princeton Offense" because I felt it fit our personnel and we could recruit to that system. I hired Larry Mangino, who learned that system at the Air Force Academy under Joe Scott. Larry never worked for me, but I knew him a long time. He joined our staff, and I gave him free rein to install the system, with good success.

NUGGET:

- "The only sign of future behavior is past behavior." —Dr. Chris Carr

FIRE RIGHT

Letting a person go is never easy. It impacts their families. It is emotional and taxing. But when it needs to be done, you have to execute it as quickly and professionally as possible. The way you let someone go says a great deal about you. If respect is one of your core values, there is no better time to show it than when you are relieving a staff member from their job. Giving them fair severance and an opportunity to "resign" is the respectful thing to do.

The longer you let a decision linger, the more it creates a negative impact on the culture of your organization.

You must document yearly and quarterly reviews with your staff, along with follow-up emails from ad hoc meetings. This memorializes any items you may need when you let someone go. It also protects the organization from lawsuits. When I got to SMU, we were forced to do yearly reviews and document them. At first, I didn't like it because it was another thing added to my workload. But as we engaged in the process, I found it very useful because it gave me an opportunity to have authentic conversations with my staff. I learned more about their goals and frustrations and how they felt we could improve the program. I also believe it was an opportunity for them to "learn and grow." It also created clarity for them on how I wanted things done in the organization.

Yearly reviews shouldn't be the only time you discuss performance with your staff. When I witnessed a behavior from a staff member that I didn't think fit our culture, I addressed it. Then I would document it for the year-end review. The last thing I wanted was to have a year-end review and mention something that happened six months prior, but was never brought to their attention. That is poor leadership.

This consistent and clear communication regarding expectations and behaviors is a must so when there is a time to remove a staff member, there should be no real surprise as to why they didn't measure up.

EMOTIONAL INTELLIGENCE

"Connect with the heart."
–MATT DOHERTY

Human nature is a funny thing. People aren't robots. We want them to be, but it is amazing how a team can lose by fifty-three points and then beat the same team by twelve points a few weeks later, as we did my last year at UNC. Human beings are individually wrapped in a body of complex wiring. No two are alike, but everyone I coached had a heart and that is where the connection must lie.

When I got to Notre Dame, I felt it wasn't as important to be liked by the players as long as they respected me. But as I developed as a leader, I started to believe that you need your people to like you first. They may respect your title, but for the relationship to grow into a commitment of the core values of RTCP, your team needs to like you first. Without that foundation, they won't move to respecting you. They won't open up their hearts to trust you and they definitely won't be committed to your mission statement. "Like" is the on-ramp to the RTC highway!

How do you connect with the heart? Some people have a knack for it. Some may need to work at it. The key is being authentic. Be you. If you try to fake it, your team will see right through it. Plus, it will be very taxing trying to be something you are not.

"Walk the floor." Visit with your staff in their offices. Make it casual. No agenda. Know the names of their spouses/partners and children. This shows you care, and it will be less intimidating than having them come to your office. You develop a trust by talking "with them" and not "at them." It is an investment of time, but this investment will pay off.

One of my favorite moments as a coach was when I took over at SMU. My first semester there I was walking the beautiful campus checking on a few classes to make sure my players were in attendance. I bumped into Jon Killen. He was a junior, but hadn't played much his first two years. We ended up sitting down and talking. He asked, "Can a player still be a leader if he doesn't play a lot?" I said, "Absolutely!" I went on to share my feelings about leadership and that anyone on a team can lead, whether you play a lot or don't play at all! Jon not only was one of the best leaders I coached, but he ended up starting, was our leading scorer as a senior and was named All-Conference Third-Team.

At Kansas, we had player mailboxes organized in the back near the coaches' offices. We encouraged the players to check their mailboxes each day. This was done intentionally.

We wanted the foot traffic of the players so when we would see them in the hall, we would have a chance to visit outside of practice. Five minutes could have a big impact on a relationship.

Nicknames are a great way to connect with someone. I love giving nicknames, as long as they have a positive connotation. As shared earlier, I gave Martin Ingelsby the nickname "Stockton." He liked it and responded to it. It enhanced our relationship.

The challenge with nicknames is that you don't want to get too "buddy-buddy" with people you have rank over. It may be confusing to a player if you are their buddy in the office, then thirty minutes later, you are yelling at him in practice. That behavior is not consistent and breaks the trust you are trying to develop.

At SMU, we had a great locker room that included a lounge area. In it was a ping-pong table. It became a terrific way for the players and coaches to connect. We even had a doubles tournament one time!

Symbolism is a tool that has been used for centuries in the military, creating a sense of being a part of a special group. It develops pride and commitment. The challenge coins noted earlier are a prime example of symbolism. They are an easy and inexpensive way to promote your core values and mission statement.

At UNC, we had a special handshake with Coach Guthridge. Every former player knows it. We never revealed it. It makes people feel a part of a special club, a fraternity ... The Carolina Family.

Consistency is the key. Coach Smith always said, "Start how you finish." If you decide to use a special handshake, do it all the time. If you decide to use challenge coins, carry them at all times. Once you become inconsistent with these things, you immediately devalue them. Do not take these things lightly. My staff and I would meet about things like the challenge coins for hours before we implemented them.

Make it fun when possible. This was hard for me. I was a grinder, but as my Myers-Briggs assessment stated only 2 percent of people think like I do. I was afraid to take my "foot off the gas" in practice. I wanted practice to hum along with a high level of energy. I decided to delegate fun. Assistant Lance Irvin would often be allotted eight minutes at the end of practice. It would be listed on the practice plan as "Irvin Time." Lance got to do any fun drill with the team that was competitive. The losing team would have to do something silly like carry the winning team the length of the court on their backs. Most players dread practice. I wanted the players to go into the locker room after practice with a smile on their faces. I sat on the sidelines in amazement. Here are these big and strong athletes who look like men, but they are laughing and cutting up like little kids. We all have a little kid inside of us!

NUGGETS:

- "Praise the actions you want repeated." —Dean Smith.

- Confidence is an amazing thing, even for experienced adults. A word of encouragement can go a long way!

TRAIN

"Tell me and I forget, teach me and
I may remember, involve me and I learn."
—BENJAMIN FRANKLIN

If you hire a new staff member and you don't onboard them properly, you are setting everyone up for frustration and failure. Training shows a commitment to your people and organization and will lead to better productivity.

Customized and personalized training helps develop the skills necessary to make your team the best it can be. I look at it like this. Imagine if I was coaching at UNC. It was the official start of practice on October 15 and we were scheduled to play at Duke on February 3. In that first practice, I installed our offensive and defensive sets and put the team through some shooting drills. At the conclusion of practice, we gathered at half court and I said to the team, "Okay, we play at Duke on February 3. See you there. Be ready to play!" That is what you are doing if you aren't training your team. You are setting everyone up for failure.

Training must include simulations. Former NBA coach Kevin Eastman often says, "You must be there before you get there." We trained our teams for game situations all the time. Dean Smith was a master of "special situations." UNC had many legendary comebacks during his reign as coach. Situations like being down two with two seconds on the clock and your team had one free throw. We called that "Archie," and Coach had a hand signal for it. These were practiced on a regular basis, so when the situation arose in a game, Coach would smile and say, "Well, we have practiced this situation before. Wouldn't it be fun to go out, execute, and win the game!" There was no panic. There was no chaos. It was just a sense of calm and confidence that carried over to his players.

NUGGETS:

- "Learning never exhausts the mind."—Leonardo da Vinci

Matt Doherty

- "For the things we have to learn before we can do them, we learn by doing them." —Aristotle

MEASURE

"If you can't measure it, you can't manage it!"
—PETER DRUCKER

"Business is a team sport," and in sports, we keep score. Whatever can be measured should be measured. It is the only way to make progress. With all the data available to us now, measuring shouldn't be a problem; however, choosing what to measure is critical. Measuring the wrong metric or measuring too many metrics can backfire. As with anything, you need to meet with your staff and decide what's important in driving the behavior you desire for your team to be successful. Then you need to make sure you stick with utilizing this metric. This goes back to mission statements. You may want to consult with a senior employee to get their thoughts. This may provide you with a critical perspective you didn't think of, plus he or she will feel respected, trusted, and committed to seeing the strategy become successful. It's a beautiful thing when you see everything flow from the core values and mission statements.

Consistency! If you start measuring a metric with enthusiasm, only to stop after a month or so, you will create confusion and lose credibility with your team.

As a player at UNC, we had "plus points." It was a system that gave you a point for certain behaviors in practice or games that Coach Smith and the staff deemed important to winning. If a player dove on the floor in practice, Coach Smith

198

would say, "Doherty. First to the floor." Then a student manager would log the "plus point" into my account.

The day after every game, Coach and his staff "graded tape." They would take about three hours to study the game from the night before. One assistant had a sheet with several categories that included defense, assist:turnover ratio, drawn charges, screens, hustle, deflections, blocked shots, and good plays. As the coaches studied the film, they might call out, "Good defense—Jordan. Assist—Black. Blocked shot—Perkins. Screen—Doherty. Good play—Worthy." An assistant would log all the plays and total up the scores. That afternoon, we would have a team meeting to go over the grades from the film, then watch some clips. The top three players with the most points in each category would get "plus points." The award winner got three points, the second-place winner got two, and the third-place winner got one. The award winners would then have their names listed on a big whiteboard in the team room for everyone to see.

The points accumulated in your account could be used to get out of sprints at the end of practice. One point per sprint. Graduating players could gift their "plus points" to an underclassman upon graduation.

What a concept! It didn't cost any money. There was no real monetary value, but it greatly impacted behavior … and winning!

We used the "plus point" system at Kansas, Notre Dame, UNC, FAU, and SMU.

MOTIVATE

If you hire right, motivation should not be a problem, but even the most driven people need motivation.

I believe most competitive people don't work hard for money. They work hard to see their name at the top of the list. Plain and simple. You could give me money for coming in first place in a contest, but given the option, I want my name at the top of a list. I want everyone to see it.

At UNC, I knew I could win the game awards for best defender, good plays, hustle, drawn charges, assist:turnover ratio and screens. I wanted to hear Coach Smith call my name. I wanted to see my name on the whiteboard in the team room. I wanted everyone else to see my name there, too. Coach recruited competitive players, and competitive people want to win … at anything.

Notice that Coach Smith never gave "plus points" to a player for scoring points in a game. No way! Scoring was a byproduct of doing all the little things like passing, screening, and executing. We stressed team basketball.

Share your vision on a regular basis and change up the routine. You meet with your team at the beginning of the year to share your vision of winning big games, league titles, and championships. I would remind them of our vision for the team and that if we were going to achieve these goals, we needed to bring great energy to the floor each and every day.

There are "dog days" of the year where things become stale and routine. As a player and coach, I always felt this in late January. Practice had been going on for several months. It's winter and we have been traveling. You could feel a lack of energy. With that, I would often change up practice. Make it shorter, change up drills, or play music during a portion of it. We would surprise the team and take a random day off. Keep the team fresh. More isn't always better! I liked to make a January hi-lite film showing the players making great plays to music. This energized the team and gave them a shot of confidence.

Malcolm Farmer was a manager for me at Notre Dame and served as my assistant at FAU and SMU. He is currently the president of the Texas Legends in the NBA's G League. He shared the concept of the "motivational toolbox." There are many tools in your motivational toolbox. You can use pliers to pull people toward success or use a hammer to hit people over the head. Both may get results, but the pliers create a strong emotional bond that will last forever.

Create "enemies." Who is doubting you? Play the disrespect card. This rallies the troops, as it did when my Notre Dame didn't make the NCAA Tournament. I quickly challenged them that the NCAA disrespected us by overlooking us. They didn't think we were good enough, and we needed to show them they made a mistake. We ended up making it all the way to the finals of the NIT!

ACCOUNTABILITY

Don't be afraid to hold your staff accountable for their performance. They need this to grow. The top performers want to be held accountable. They are competitive people and they know if everyone is held accountable, there will be a level playing field to be judged against. Plus, by creating a culture of accountability, the top performers won't feel dragged down by low performers. Many people leave companies for more than money. Many high performers leave a company when they feel they have to carry too much of the workload for the company to be successful. Why do you see NBA players joining up with other great players?

Additionally, you need to hold yourself accountable. You probably had more to do with a failure than you care to admit. Roy would often say, "If you are pointing a finger at someone else, there are three fingers pointing back at you." When you make a mistake, own it and share it with your team. This will show them you are human and authentic.

I had the primary role in my demise at UNC. The more time passed, the more I realize that I was in control of many of the issues that arose. I had to own that and "learn and grow" from it.

FAILURE

"Success consists of going from failure
to failure without loss of enthusiasm."
—WINSTON CHURCHILL

Embrace failure. Celebrate failure. Sounds crazy? I love John Maxwell's book *Failing Forward*. I studied in John's program and learned a great deal. He states, "The difference between average people and achieving people is their perception and response to failure." John says, "Make failure your friend."

My brother, John, and I had many a talks about this. John is a successful executive at Goldman Sachs in NYC and played college basketball at the United States Merchant Marine Academy. John was a great player there and very competitive. In the private wealth business, you deal with a lot of rejection as you call on wealthy people, and you're lucky if they give you five minutes. In addition, he started working just as 9-11 happened. Pink slips were showing up everywhere. We talked about how we were used to failing. As a player and coach, you fail often, and your job is to "study the tape" and get better.

How do you react to failure? I love Mandela's quote at the beginning of this chapter, "I never lose. I either win or learn." The more we fail, the more we learn. The more we learn, the better we get. The better we get, the closer we are to reaching our destiny. That sounds like Thomas Edison, "I have not failed. I've just found ten thousand ways that won't work."

You cannot have a culture where people are afraid to fail. By creating a safe environment for your team, their creativity will flourish and the energy within the organization with grow. Your company may fail more than it succeeds, but it only takes one! One what? One new client! One new deal! One new employee! One new patent! One new idea! One key recruit!

NUGGETS:

"Successful failures":

- Abraham Lincoln lost his job at the age of twenty-three. Lost many elections in the State of Illinois.

- Albert Einstein failed the entrance exam into school at sixteen. Sold insurance after struggling in college.

- Bill Belichick was fired by the Browns after five seasons in his first attempt as a head coach.

- Elvis Presley was told he couldn't sing, so he started driving a truck.

- Joe Torre was fired by the Mets after five years in his first attempt at managing.

- Michael Jordan was famously cut by the varsity coach as a sophomore in high school.

- Oprah Winfrey ran away from home at thirteen and became pregnant at 14 and lost her TV anchor job after college.

- Steven Spielberg was rejected by USC's film school for poor grades.

- Walt Disney was fired by the Kansas City Star for not having any imagination.

- Winston Churchill lost five elections, battled depression, and had a severe lisp.

- Vincent van Gogh sold just one painting during his lifetime.

ETHICS

"Truth is one of the casualties of our culture."
—Bob McKillop

People lie, cheat, steal, and then deny everything in front of God and everyone! It is a sad commentary on life. Ethics have eroded. I believe we have become more materialistic and less moralistic. Why? The demise of the family unit? The lack of discipline in schools? Lack of religion and God being taught? Entitlement culture? Comparison games on social media? Trying to live a Hollywood lifestyle? Will it get worse before it gets better? How do we improve ethics in our country?

I don't have the answer. This is a cultural thing that needs to be developed at the core.

LOYALTY

"A thousand enemies outside the house are better than one within."
—Arab proverb

It is critical to surround yourself with people who are loyal to you and your success. People who put you in position for success need to be rewarded with your loyalty. However, blind loyalty can be shortsighted.

I took my staff with me from Notre Dame and replaced the assistants at Carolina. I was showing loyalty to my staff who helped me have a good year at Notre Dame. I wasn't going to leave them out on the street. However, by bringing them to UNC in that situation, I put them in harm's way. I put us all in harm's way. Yes, I showed loyalty, but I put us all on the hot seat.

Looking back, I should have taken my time, consulted my "Personal Board of Directors," discussed it with Dick Baddour and Coach Smith, and come up with a plan. The timing of the hire didn't lend itself to taking my time, but these are the decisions that can make or break an organization. The plan I should have executed would have been to keep the UNC staff in place while offering my staff positions in the UNC program at the same salaries they were making in South Bend. My staff may not have liked it, but they wouldn't be left on the street and I would have been protecting them, whether they knew it or not. Coach Smith, the former players, the fans, the players, and the secretaries … they all would have been happier and maybe I would still be the coach in Chapel Hill.

NUGGET:

- "You can teach someone how to defend the pick and roll, but you can't teach them to love you." —Larry Brown

MANAGING CHANGE

"Few things are more important during a change event than communication from leaders who can paint a clear and confidence-inspiring vision of the future."
—SARAH CLAYTON

Know your environment and its history. Study it.

Looking back, I realize that I should have gone slower with all the changes I made at UNC. I made drastic changes that were embraced at Notre Dame. UNC may have needed similar changes, but with the success UNC had for decades, the changes I made were viewed as being disrespectful of the program. This change was difficult for many people, especially the support staff who I inherited. There were five administrative assistants. Four of them had been there for about an average of twenty-five years each. Even though I played at UNC and was part of "The Family," this change was traumatic for them because they were close to the former staff. I brought in a whole new set of coaches, along with changing the physical layout of the offices and locker room. Now, I can only imagine how they felt.

In addition, all the former players who were in the "Carolina Family" were dealing with the drastic changes that were taking place in "their program." They all had long-time relationships with the former coaches and the administrative assistants. It was a shock to their systems as well.

If I had to do it over again, I would have kept the previous staff in place, as I noted above.

Try to understand the true motives of the people you are dealing with. Most people are motivated by self-preservation. Drastic change is difficult for people to handle, especially if they have been in a position for a long time. In the DISC assessment, 69 percent of the population are "Ss". They like a "steady" environment.

I had worked with executive coach Dr. Jerry Bell. He suggests, "Don't make any change within twenty-five feet of someone's desk without their input." People need to be included in the process of change, and when they're not, they feel disrespected. I broke that rule. I wish I had worked with Dr. Bell BEFORE I took the job!

I should have taken the time to visit with the administrative staff and not gone out recruiting right away. This would have shown them that I respected them and valued them as people. I should have leaned on them for input because they were such a critical part of the program.

If I had to do it again, I would allow Coach Smith to manage the tickets and parking passes however he wanted. I should have asked for a small allotment to accommodate the needs of me and my staff. Tickets were a valuable commodity and I pulled that from him. He felt disrespected in this process and I believe it was a big mistake on my part.

I should have hired Eddie Fogler as a consultant. As a former assistant at UNC and savvy head coach, he understood Coach Smith and the Carolina program as well as anyone. He could have guided me through the challenges that I was dealing with.

NUGGETS

- "Powerful and sustained change requires constant communication, not only throughout the rollout but after the major elements of the plan are in place. The more kinds of communication employed, the more effective they are."
  —DeAnne Aguirre

- "If you are entrusted with bringing about change, you likely possess the knowledge needed to advance the organization, and you might have a plan—but knowledge is not enough. You have to bring yourself to each interaction in a deeply authentic way. People don't care how much you know until they know how much you care." —Doug Conant

- "Change cannot be put on people. The best way to instill change is to do it with them. Create it with them." —Lisa Bodell

- "The people must have ownership in the vision. They need to be enabled to accomplish it. If there is one investment you should make, it is in people." —Modesta Lilian Mbughuni

MANAGING UP

"Managing bottom-up change is its own art."
—Kevin Kelly

Managing up means you aren't the boss. Just because your title says "boss" doesn't always mean you are.

Since Dick Baddour was the athletic director at UNC, he was my formal boss. He was my "flowchart boss." Dick had a great disposition and years of experience on me, so there wasn't much "managing up" that needed to be done. He was authentic and listened to my input when he asked questions. I truly like Dick and his wife, Lynda. He has a leadership academy named after him at UNC. What a great opportunity for the students. I know my daughter, Hattie, has learned a great deal there.

There are bosses who are informal bosses, "off the flowchart bosses." Dean Smith was my "off the flowchart boss." There was no organizational chart with his name on it, but he cast a big shadow over the athletic department. I am sure Dick had to deal with a lot of that, too.

Embrace legacy leaders and celebrate them. Include them in the process and make them feel welcomed in the organization. It is not the leader's program. The program belongs to all the stakeholders. I remember a time when one of Coach Smith's friends called me and said, "You need to call Coach Smith more." It felt odd hearing that. I didn't want to bother him. He was retired. Plus, I wasn't always comfortable talking to him, just like when I was a player meeting him in his office. Those were somewhat intimidating experiences. However, I understood that UNC basketball was a huge part of his life for forty years. When Coach Guthridge took over, Coach Smith kept his office and Coach Guthridge continued to work out of his. With the staff changes and new blood in the office, I see that Coach felt disconnected. My lack of emotional intelligence was evident.

A time I did call Coach, I sought his political advice. It was an election year and I knew nothing about politics. I remember calling him from my car to get his thoughts. He was a devoted Democrat and a huge civil rights advocate. In 1959, Assistant Coach Dean Smith joined Rev. Seymour for lunch with a black student at The Pines Restaurant to help integrate Chapel Hill! He then recruited the first African-American student-athlete in the history of UNC, named Charlie Scott. I remember asking Coach his thoughts on the election and the pros and cons of each candidate. He said, "You know the Democratic Party is focused on helping people, especially people from disadvantaged backgrounds." He was pushing the Democratic ticket pretty hard!

HONOR THE PAST

As a leader, it is important to show respect for the past. That includes the past leaders who sat in your chair and were a part of building that organization. It's the right thing to do. It builds equity with all the stakeholders and creates goodwill for you and the brand.

Larry Brown took over for me at SMU. I was there for six years. We were close to turning the corner, but never quite did. When Coach Brown took over, he praised me for leaving him good players and building the foundation for the success his teams had on the court. It was flattering. I remember telling him after his second or third season at SMU, "Coach, I really appreciate all the nice things you say about me, but you don't need to do that anymore."

WELLNESS

Mental health is real. Emotional support is critical. I thank God for a strong wife and good friends. You need to surround yourself with people who love you for the PERSON you are, not the title you have.

Managing the stress of working in the current times of modern technology makes work/life balance very difficult. You feel you can't escape work. It's not healthy, but I am a guilty party. We took a vacation to Holden Beach, NC, this summer and I was on my phone and iPad the whole time. I had FOMO—Fear of Missing Out. Since I am self-employed now, I don't have anyone to delegate to. If I don't do it, it doesn't get done, but we all still need to unplug.

Delegate. Give your staff responsibilities that you don't have to manage. Coach them on how you would like things to be handled and trust them to deal with those things. This allows them to grow as leaders and takes some things off your plate.

Talk to a professional. It is hard to clear your head when your heart is broken. Professionals know how to get to the root of your emotional issues and help you put things in the proper perspective.

Triggers. There are many triggers that may get the best of you. Do your best to avoid them and/or pivot from them quickly. Obsessing on past events that brought you anguish is not healthy! Forgiveness will help you manage these triggers.

Don't compare yourself to others who may seem to have it better than you. Run your own race.

NUGGETS:

- "Anger turned inward leads to depression." —Fran Johnston

- "If someone can do the job 80 percent as well as you, let them handle the task."

- "Comparison games are the work of the devil!"

- "Comparison is the act of violence against the self." — lyanla Vanzant

- "Comparison is the thief of joy." —Theodore Roosevelt

- "Let people work to the top of their job description." — Dr. James McNabb

- Leave your cell phone in the car when you go out to eat with family and friends.

- "It is good to laugh." —Mary Doherty

- Organize. You either manage your day or your day will manage you.

- Learn how to say "no." You don't have to take every request.

- Coach your "gatekeepers" to manage your requests. Have an assistant who can filter the demands on your time.

- Eat well and exercise. This relieves stress and gives you the foundation to make sound decisions. (I stink at this!)

"LEARN AND GROW"

"You will be the same person in five years as you are today except for the people you meet and the books you read."
–CHARLIE "TREMENDOUS" JONES

Read. I have enjoyed reading much more in my adult life than I did as a young man. Books on leadership and history are my favorites. I buy more audiobooks now since I am in my car a great deal. Instead of listening to music or sports, I find it fascinating to learn in my car.

Network. Join a civic group. Put yourself in position to meet new people who have success in various fields. As a coach, I loved attending clinics to learn from other coaches and develop new relationships. I joined the John Maxwell Team and attended their conference in Orlando, FL.

ADVERSITY

"Life is not fair. Get used to it."
—BILL GATES

I was proud of the way I emotionally managed the 8-20 season. I never placed blame on the players or the previous staff. A leader needs to be out front and handle criticism in a professional manner. You have to lead with grace in times of adversity and you need to show strength.

I tried to follow these guidelines:

- Don't hide

- Be honest without embarrassing anyone

- Control the narrative

- Develop a well-thought-out plan with key advisors

- Communicate the plan with a touch of hope for a better day

Stay positive during setbacks. When Sean May got hurt in 2003, I didn't panic. It was "next man up," and we won the very next game only two nights later. People are watching and they will follow your lead.

Temperament is such an important part of leadership. The ability to stay calm in the face of adversity is a challenge for many of us, but it can be developed. You have to be like an actor on Broadway.

Looking back, I should have managed the team after our loss to Georgetown. Maybe I would have still been forced to resign, but I may have had more control of the situation.

Control the narrative in bad times. People will create their own narrative if you don't take charge of it.

I should have attended the press conference. If I had been present, it would have been difficult for the press conference to turn negative about my leadership.

Compassion. Sometimes, we show more compassion to others than we do to ourselves.

Understand you are not defined by your success in your chosen field. On your death bed, you will be defined by the type of life you led and the impact you made on the people and communities you touched along the way.

People talk about the boss. You have to be secure in your own skin. Whether you like it or not, people will gather in small groups and talk about you.

Manage the noise. Compartmentalize things so you can focus on the present. This is easier said than done, but it is critical to stay in the present and not let stress impact decisions or your health.

Perspective. I think it is critical to put things in perspective in the face of adversity. I carried a military coin in my pocket given to me by Lieutenant Colonel Matt Karres. Matt was from Chapel Hill and served in several wars. I learned a lot of leadership lessons from him. When I was faced with a tough loss or a difficult season, I was able to say to myself, "It could be worse. I could be in Afghanistan." I would often say to my team after a setback that if this is the worst thing you face in your life, you will lead a charmed life. Sports teaches you many lessons.

Your Rolodex will get cleared out when you fail. Some people won't call when you lose your job. You thought you had a lot of friends, but 75 percent of them will not reach out to you when you fail. Why? Some people don't know what to say and others were friends with your position, not with you! This can be therapeutic because now you know who your true friends are. I still remember who called me … and who didn't!

Adversity will test your faith. I choose to lean on God.

NUGGETS:
- "So what! Now what!" —Principal Linda Cliatt-Wayman

- "Trust in the Lord with all your heart, and do not lean on your own understanding. In all your ways acknowledge him, and he will make straight your paths." –Proverbs 3:5-6 ESV

- "Take the high road, there is less traffic up there!" —Dr. Kevin White

- "It is easy to become bitter but try to get better. People don't like to be around negative people."

- "Look through the front windshield, not the rearview mirror."

- "Victory has a thousand fathers, but defeat is an orphan." —John F. Kennedy

- "Compassion and grace come from inner strength. It is not a sign of weakness if the leader is secure with him or herself."

SUCCESS

"Flattery is all right so long as you don't inhale."
—ADLAI STEVENSON

Coach Smith was always gracious in victory. He would praise the other team and always give credit to his players, especially the seniors. He showed tremendous class and dignity. Coach K and Bob McKillop both showed compassion in victories over my UNC teams. It is just the right thing to do as a leader.

As a head coach at Notre Dame and UNC, I had some very successful moments. A lot of people praised me. I was on national TV and in national publications. It can be intoxicating.

Looking back, I realized that some of the attention went to my head. Ego can get the best of any human.

CONTRACT

"A dull pencil is better than a sharp mind."
—Benjamin Franklin

Hire a good lawyer. Sign a contract with the end in mind. This is hard to do with all the excitement of a new position, but this is the time you have the leverage to make sure your contract is buttoned up in the event the worst-case scenario occurs. Plan for a good ending and plan for a bad ending.

NUGGETS:
- Get all the details in writing.
- Negotiate when you have the leverage.

PIVOTING

"With an ever-increasing number of career choices, 30 percent of the workforce will now change careers or jobs every twelve months."
—Career Change Statistics

In today's workplace, you need to be prepared to pivot into a new job or career. People get fired, positions get eliminated, and companies are bought out on a regular basis. Make a list of industries that interest you and learn about them while you are in your current role.

I started out on Wall Street. I coached and got fired. Did TV and real estate. Got back into coaching and got fired. Worked for the Pacers. Worked for the A-10 Conference. Started the

Doherty Coaching Practice while also becoming a sales representative. I do two radio shows a week and I am writing a book! I would say I have had ten careers ... so far!

FINANCIAL

These are the lessons I have learned about money:

1. I wish I saved more.

2. Properly invested money will double every seven years.

3. Have enough money in savings so you can go one year without a job.

4. Live within your means.

5. Credit card debt is foolish. I have ALWAYS paid off my credit card each month!

6. Keep your debt to a minimum.

7. Find ways to create passive income. Investing in real estate is one way to increase your income stream without having to play an active role in that industry.

8. Develop relationships with people who are experts in their field and "piggyback" on their investments.

9. Use 529 accounts to save for your children's education.

10. Put the maximum allowed into your 401(k) and your IRA accounts.

11. Buy used cars.

12. "Need vs. want." Buy what you need, not what you want.

EXECUTIVE COACHING

I found it invaluable to have an executive coach. Dr. Bell worked with me at UNC. I wish I leaned on him more at that time. Since then, I have always had a person who would work with me. Someone who wasn't emotionally attached to my employer and could help me navigate the challenging seas of leadership.

Executive coaches help leaders improve their self-confidence and self-awareness. They bring a wealth of experience in dealing with success, failure, office politics and team building. A good coach listens and is a "thinking partner" that shares wisdom allowing the leader to work through the challenges that lie before them.

Being a leader can be very lonely and a good coach is a good teammate. They assist the leader. Leaders have real fears and need to be able to share those fears in a safe environment. Trust is imperative. Fears internalized lead to stress that will be felt by everyone within the organization if it is not released properly.

A good coach is a good listener. By sharing with a coach the leader can verbalize his or her thoughts and often figure out the proper course of action as their thoughts are rolling out of their mouths. When you hear yourself talk through an issue it can crystalize the problem leading you to come up with the best course of action. A good coach is often a conduit allowing you to come up with the correct solution.

As the head coach at North Carolina I often felt too busy to take the time to meet with Dr. Bell. It would have been easy to cancel an appointment due to the overwhelming amount of work that was on my desk. But every time we met I came away with some wisdom that helped me and my program become better.

Executive coaching is an investment in you and your organization that will pay tremendous dividends.

I'm available!

FORGIVENESS

"Don't allow people to rent space in your head."
—GARY COXE

Learn to forgive. Selfishly, forgiveness is the best thing one can do because it is freeing. If Jesus could forgive the men who crucified him, you can forgive people who may wrong you. If God can forgive us for all of our sins, we should be able to forgive our fellow man.

By carrying a grudge you will never be present. You will be preoccupied with resentment that will distract you from the task at hand. Resentment eats at any peace and joy you will be able to achieve. It impacts your sleep, your health and that bitterness will resonate to all those around you.

In addition to being able to forgive others you need to be able to forgive yourself. It is very difficult because leaders strive to be perfect and we are often our harshest critics. We are not perfect. We are human and humans make mistakes. Show yourself compassion. It will bring peace.

As stated earlier, there are many triggers that may get the best of you. Do your best to avoid them and/or pivot from them quickly. Obsessing on past events that brought you anguish is not healthy! Forgiveness will help you manage these triggers.

CHAPTER TWENTY-ONE:

THANK YOU

Thank you for investing your time and money in *Rebound*. It is truly humbling that you took the time to read my book. I hesitated in writing it because I didn't want people to think I had an ego. I wasn't sure if my story was worth sharing. However, enough people encouraged me to write this book that I finally accomplished it.

I want to formally thank my loving family Kelly, Tucker, and Hattie. It hasn't been easy for them over the last twenty years. Kelly continues to be tough, loving and a wonderful mother. I am very proud of Tucker. He was an All-American lacrosse player at Lake Norman High School and gave Kelly and me some fond memories watching him compete on the field and how he handled his success with grace. He played Division I lacrosse at Bellarmine University in Louisville and graduated with terrific grades. He is a gentleman. Hattie was a successful swimmer at Lake Norman High School before attending UNC on a rowing scholarship. I still remember being with her on campus her first semester. She was wearing a Carolina Blue sweatshirt standing across from Carmichael Dormitory. As she walked off toward the Bell Tower, pride filled my chest as she was walking the same red brick paths I walked on many years ago.

As I mentioned, I have put notes together for a book since I was forced from my coaching position at UNC in 2003. I started writing this book and stopped many times. It has been seventeen years of pain ... and growth for me. As I reflected on my leadership journey, not just at UNC, but at Notre Dame, FAU, and SMU, I made many mistakes that have left "coaching scars." I still make mistakes as a leader and trust I will continue to do so. My hope is that I continue to "learn and grow" and that *Rebound* inspires you to do the same.

Leadership is never fully mastered. It is a continuous journey, a journey that is exciting and fulfilling. However, we will be faced with many challenges, but let it drive us to get better each day!

I challenge you to be a lifelong learner!

RTCP!

God bless!

ABOUT THE AUTHOR

After being fired from his dream job in 2003, Matt Doherty decided to "Learn & Grow" by embarking on a leadership journey that took him to the Darden School of Business and The Wharton School. He went on to become the head coach at FAU and SMU in addition to working at ESPN, the Indiana Pacers and the Atlantic 10 Conference. He currently runs the Doherty Coaching Practice along with working in media and private business.

Matt is married to Kelly and has two children, Tucker and Hattie. They reside in Mooresville, NC.